Dear Waiting Patient, 2008
May your journey
be enlightened,
Victoria Lynn

DEAR SISTER, ONCE ABUSED

A story of hope and freedom
from the bondage of childhood sexual abuse

By

Victoria Lynn

Published by Aradiance Publishing Co.
P.O. Box 13855, Mill Creek, Washington 98082
http://www.aradiance.com

Publisher's Note: This publication is designed to provide additional tools and insight into the area of CSA and is sold with the understanding that the publisher is not engaged in rendering psychological counseling services. The remedies, approaches, and techniques described herein are meant to supplement, and not to be a substitute for, professional care or treatment. If professional expert assistance or counseling is needed, the services of a competent professional should be sought.

With the exception of health practitioners, identifying data have been changed to insure confidentiality.

First Printing 2003
Printed and bound in the United States

Victoria Lynn
Dear Sister, Once Abused: a story of hope and freedom from the bondage of childhood sexual abuse
Includes bibliographical references and index

Library of Congress Control Number: 2003090477

Cover concept and illustration, "Field of Daisies", painted by Victoria Lynn with the assistance of Valerieanne J. Skinner, author of *The World of Mirrors*. The daisies on the cover are shown, as ourselves, at various stages of growth. Heavenly rays rest upon each flower, symbolic of love and light.

ISBN 0-9715737-0-0 $16.95

This book is dedicated to all my sisters, once abused,
perhaps now tormented, with the dream that individually and as a
sisterhood, we can scatter rays of hope for the abused, embrace and
teach the captives, and shout to the skies,
"WE ARE FREE!"

Contents

Foreword–Carlfred Broderick VII
Acknowledgments IX
Preface XI
Introduction 1

I   IN THE BEGINNING 3
    1   Three Major Traumas at Age Three 4

II DISCOVERY 11
    2   My Own Discovery of Abuse 12
    3   Denial 16
    4   Flashback, Step Forward 19

III TROUBLESOME AFTER EFFECTS 25
    5   Adolescent After Effects 26
    6   Somatic Illness 33
    7   Triggers to Childhood Sexual Abuse Memories ... 43
    8   Depression 49

IV RECOVERY 53
    9   Physical Recovery 54
    10 Emotional Recovery 58
    11 Spiritual Recovery 68
    12 Therapy 71

V   FAMILY 81
    13 To Mothers 82
    14 To Fathers 88
    15 To Siblings 95
    16 To Children 98
    17 To Grandmothers 102
    18 To Perpetrator 108
    19 To Parents 112
    20 Positive Parenting Ideas 118

VI SUPPORTIVE OTHERS 123
   21 Blue Ribbon Recipients 124
   22 Friends 126
   23 Partners 128
   24 Clergy 134
   25 Mental Health Technicians 139
   26 Physicians/Therapists 141
   27 Advantages of Using Spiritual Beliefs 154

VII TRANSITION FROM VICTIM TO THRIVER 157
   28 Victim 158
   29 Survivor 161
   30 Thriver 163

The Healing Process Timetable 168
Resources 169
Bibliography/Recommended Reading 172
Index 174

Foreword

This book is about how one person has struggled with private pain. It is, in my view, a courageous and effective attempt to share what she has learned from the process that she hopes might be helpful to others, both those struggling with the issues in their own lives and those who are committed to do what they can to help others through the process.

It pleases me that the author does not stop with exploring the healing process. She pushes beyond to colonizing new frontiers of personal insight and fulfillment.

The author is herself a nurse and so brings some of the discipline and objectivity of her professional training to bear on the issues. She is a person of faith, and this healing perspective adds a depth to her story that I find missing in more clinically sterile approaches. But finally and above all, she is an honest and compassionate person dealing with a challenge, which she believes, is best met with the help of others who care.

Dr. Carlfred Broderick, Ph.D., Professor Emeritus
University of Southern California, Dept. of Sociology

Acknowledgments

My heart is full of gratitude for the people who have encouraged and supported me during each phase of this book's development. Upon hearing the topic, they have graciously volunteered their time and talents. Of particular importance was the question my mother asked, which further inspired this journey, "Honey, will you write a book so I can better understand what happened to you?"

Preface

It happened over eight years ago in a most peaceful, sacred spot in Seattle, Washington, while I was visiting my sister, Jeanne. We were enjoying beautiful music together when an unmistakable voice came to me from above. It was loud, yet soft and clear. "Victoria, write a book."

Excuses came instantly: "Why me? I don't finish things, and what would I call it?" Out of nowhere came the words: "DEAR SISTER, ONCE ABUSED." The title concerned me. First of all, I didn't want to single out women, for I wanted men to read the book also. Secondly, could I refer to all the women who may read this book as *sisters*?

Then I attended my son's graduation, where he had been chosen as a speaker. I experienced some concern, as he had not reviewed his speech with me, and he had a tendency to surprise his audience.

"Our high school is pregnant!" He opened with full volume as I slumped a little lower into my seat. "Not with one fetus, but with 214!" The analogy was meaningful, in that all the students were being "delivered" into the world at the same point as they left their high school environment. While every student was a unique individual, each had shared experiences by attending the same school together. Each had participated in similar teenage emotions, and they were joined as one group celebrating the beginning of a new life beyond high school. I then understood his provocative speech and could relax while enjoying the brief, yet powerful, message. The closing was most impressive: "And that makes brothers and sisters of us all. I love you all. Amen."

During the past twenty years, I have heard numerous heart-rending accounts related by persons young and old of their struggle with histories of mistreatment. I speak not only of those involved directly as the abused individuals, but also include those whose lives have been tainted by having a grandmother, mother, sister, aunt or dear friend who suffered the rippling effects of their sexual abuse. As with my son's graduating classmates, these individuals had various religious and racial differences, yet shared a common bond.

I firmly believe each of us share a tremendous challenge, not only to discover our wholeness (some call this recovering or healing), but also to break the victim cycle and to assist others in their quest. In using my son's analogy, I maintain these factors make sisters of us all. Thus, the title, "Dear Sister, Once Abused," is my call to the many women I consider my sisters.

Introduction

In writing my story, I have no desire to seek revenge or hurt anyone. My hope is to further educate people in the reality of and recovery from CSA (childhood sexual abuse). Ignorance about this topic can be damaging and dangerous. Unfortunately, my story is far from unique. It is detailed, personal, and as far as I know, complete enough. At times, telling it has been helpful for others as well as myself. It is not about secrets. It is not about shame. I have spent most of my years here on earth feeling unsure of myself and with a fair amount of dread in wondering what else bad would happen to me. I have learned to pay more attention to pleasant moments and fresh dreams. I prefer to look for good things, and in writing this book many have come down from heaven in small and miraculous ways.

Professionally, I am a registered nurse who has worked for a number of years in mental health areas. Always drawn to the patients suffering from depression with backgrounds of trauma, I felt a challenge to assist them in positive self-discovery and useful life skills. I am not an expert in the area of sexual abuse. The ground has so recently been broken in this complex area that efforts to improve understanding and treatment are in process. There is still much to be discovered and developed. My main credential remains my own experience because I have been there and back again. It has taken years to be able to relate my abuse experience without trembling, and even more years of recovery to be willing to say to an audience, "Yes, this happened to me,"

It is important for readers to realize that my account, as with all hidden memories, is likely distorted to some degree (during flashbacks, I view the world through the eyes of a three year old child) and certainly fragmented (I've received only bits and pieces of my abuse picture). It is my truth, as I know it. I have done my best to be as accurate as possible. If my story, given in parts as it appears on these pages, can be useful, then I have realized an additional purpose in my suffering and recovery. I can then say as Mahatma Gandhi said, "My life is my message."

Most authors suggest you read their book from beginning to end.

Due to this book's sensitive topic, I'm giving my readers permission to read the final chapter on thriving first.

Why? Because reading my story can cause discomfort. It involves following a journey that connects one with human suffering and awakens awareness of that part of us that resists knowing. The journey will be worth it, for it dispels ignorance, and opens hearts to understanding. If you need a break while reading this book's intense areas, you may also 'peek ahead' to lighter segments such as found in my rappelling adventure, p.60, "Recapturing Delight", p. 64, and "I Am a Treasure", p. 66, etc. You may also choose to read this book slowly, one segment at a time.

Because the abuse that happened to me lacked recognition, intervention and therapy while I was a child, suffering and healing were drawn out for many years. Just as the flowering daisy on the cover, it has taken time for me to blossom, to open myself to the rays of hope and love. No longer is my life haunted by nightmares, major flashbacks or crippling anxiety and depression.

Before you read THE BEGINNING, be assured that there is a HAPPY ENDING to this book.

I

IN THE BEGINNING

"From the very beginning Victoria smiled a lot, was a happy baby, and as she grew she always made me think of sunshine. I remember when she was only one year old I made her a new coat and hat, and the only color that seemed right was a beautiful, clear, sunny yellow. I embroidered daisies on the collar, and I was so proud when everyone admired her in the new creation."

Victoria's mother

Chapter 1

Three Major Traumas at Age Three

My third year was rough all around. My therapist, Ann, used to tell me it was at the tender age of three that I determined completely and unconditionally to survive. With my second and third trauma I could have surrendered, not only to despondency, but to death during that formative year.

Psychologically, age three is the year of settling, following the so-called "Terrible Twos." An important childhood function is to establish trust. My third year taught me just the opposite. It taught me that I could trust no one, that life was incredibly unpredictable and frightening, and that only by pretending could I find an escape. I survived three major traumas that year.

The Accident

Mom witnessed the truck accident while talking on the phone. It was terrifying for her to see me chase after a neighbor boy right into the path of an oncoming truck. Helpless, she watched the impact, and then ran out to hold her screaming little girl while awaiting arrival of an ambulance. My head wound was bleeding profusely, but what bothered my mother most were my screams. When help arrived at the scene, she commented to the emergency technician how awful it was to have her little girl screaming so wildly in pain. He comforted her with, "Ma'am, a lot of children we come to help aren't screaming.

You are a lucky one. Just let her scream and be glad she is alive and conscious."

Mother was there for me from the moment of her first embrace. I remember holding onto my stuffed dog, Skippy, as the doctor stitched my forehead. My parents made sure I had my dog to hold. There was a newspaper article written about the accident, and a great deal of increased love and appreciation for a saved life. I learned to stop and look both ways before crossing the street. Other than a thickened scar across my hairline, my recovery was complete and uneventful.

The Sexual Abuse

The second trauma, in contrast to the first, was not newsworthy, nor followed with increased love and attention. There was no comfort, no holding, and no grieving parent to share the pain. It was not an accident, yet it would mar my life for the next forty-five years and mark me as a victim of abuse. It is my hope that you, the reader, will be able to believe the unbelievable. Believing what happened to me will help you be able to believe it happens to other little children. Before we can solve a problem, we must recognize and accept that it does exist.

My favorite person on earth was my father's mother. Nana saw me as clever, smart, capable and hers. She had claimed me at birth because she did not want to be slighted. The other set of grandparents had claimed my first-born sister, so I was raised knowing I was Nana's favorite grandchild. I spent a great deal of time in her home absorbing her tough, yet fun-loving lifestyle, delighting in the freedom I felt there. I played, hiked and took risks, such as daring to go to the edge of the roof of her two story home.

One disadvantage in visiting Grandma was that she did not live alone. Although Grandpa was out of town a lot, as well as in and out of the marriage, at times he was around spoiling our fun with his demands and criticisms. I never did like the man. He sometimes called Grandma a "Dumb Dame". Nothing she did was good enough. He became especially furious when Grandma would accidentally burn his food–she didn't talk back much but regularly burned his toast. When he would rant and rave, I would hide in a cubbyhole by the heater.

It seemed to irritate him that Grandma spoiled me so. He would yell, "You'd do anything for Victoria. Why, if she wanted to be in the sunshine and didn't want to go outside, you would take the roof off for her." This prospect sounded good to me, although it didn't make a whole lot of sense. But then, Grandpa rarely made sense. Grandpa had a history of belligerence that his family could not beat out of him. He was known as the family rebel, yet he served in World War I and was a successful businessperson. He used to give my sisters and me silver dollars, which he would encourage us to save, and I remember his favorite saying was, "We get smart too late and old too soon." However, my main memory of him was that he was extremely crude. His wet kisses were sickening. He often told off-color jokes (most of which I did not understand), and he had a large calendar inside his closet featuring a nude Marilyn Monroe. He took me to see *The Seven Year Itch*, her big movie sensation, and insisted we sit through it twice.

The Trips

When I was four years old, my mother and I went on a trip to visit my dad at the Laramie building site where Grandpa had a construction project. Quite regularly, Grandma would visit him at his various long term building sites. Grandpa and Dad worked as partners on many construction jobs. Paramount in my mind is the apartment in which they stayed. I remember so clearly the details of that horrid basement with the green leather stools. It was dark and dreary with pinewood walls and army blankets on the beds. I still shudder when I recall visiting that apartment as a four-year-old. I vividly remember feeling terrified and unable to sleep at night. I saw the shadow of a police officer at the window, and I believed he was going to get me. I screamed that there was a man in my room. I threw the covers over my head, scooted down to the footboard in an attempt to hide, and then I screamed that the man was under the covers, too! Mother spent the night sleeping with me, but her efforts to comfort me were fruitless. The terror did not relent. I could not eat on that trip and I became physically ill. I truly believe I was revisiting the scene of a previous crime. Although not within my conscious awareness, the clues were undeniable.

So many of my childhood memories are absent. When I attempt to recall what happened to me in the area of abuse, only the Laramie visit at age four stands out. In assembling my history, I asked my mother if I had ever been to that Laramie apartment before age four. "Oh, yes," she recalled. "You went with your grandma to visit when you were three." It was not unusual for me to accompany Grandma; however, one fateful visit turned out to be outrageously unusual.

On trips with Grandma, she indulged me with coloring books, paper dolls, yummy treats, and anything I wanted at restaurants. I kept active and, like any three-year-old, I did not want to go to bed at night. Covered in the blackness of night, my grandfather entered my room and raped me.

While he was in the act, my grandmother entered the room. I heard her exclaim, "Wilma (my mother's name) will kill you if she finds out!" Being three, I assumed Grandma was talking to me. Thus, the perceived threat of death effectively sealed the secret in my mind. In addition to the pain, shock, and terror, it added another dimension to my personal hell. My most dreadful and confusing nightmare surfaced years later. In it, I would see my own mother coming at me with bared teeth and a long knife. I would wake up cold, sick, and confused. This theme did not appear in my conscious mind again until thirty-eight years later. Following that horrid night, most of my nightmares would be of raging, out-of-control fires that would finally force me to the edge of a nearby cliff.

Why didn't I dream of the actual abuse? I have come to believe it is because the act was so horrendous that my mind buried the event, a means by which my consciousness protected me. From my encounters with many other victims of sexual abuse, I have also come to believe that some future event, usually in adulthood, can open the door for the earlier trauma to come forward. The fear was so intense and real, my child's mind transformed it into something more acceptable. Being consumed by fire was how my unconscious portrayed the abuse. The act of sexual abuse was not within my capability as a child to conceptualize. I also remember having nightmares about police officers searching for me, and dreams of a large man entering my bedroom. Even as I grew older, I could not understand why I was having such nightmares.

Protection?

Grandma's reaction, typical of that era, was to ignore the whole issue and to pretend it had never happened. Thus, Grandpa was protected, and her freedom to spend time with her favorite granddaughter was not threatened. I honestly believe she thought it would be best for me if I could forget the whole matter as quickly as possible. Grandma was never a touching, holding, hugging type, and I have reasons to believe there was no attempt to console me after she discovered Grandpa in my room that night. I do not think either of my grandparents had a clue concerning the devastation the events of that night would have upon me. I also believe Grandma tried to make it clear to Grandpa that the act would not be repeated. On subsequent visits, Grandma always had me sleep with her in the master bedroom. If Grandpa was home, he slept in a bedroom upstairs. Grandma knelt and prayed with me every night. I liked those times, because she seemed strong and protective.

People with sincere intent have asked me, "Do you really believe, Victoria, that having been abused in this way just once was enough to cause the damage you have suffered?" My answer is "YES." I remind them that because my childhood memories are so few, abuse in one form or another may have continued beyond this one experience. However, this brutal assault was an ending of innocence, of believing in myself, of my trusting in being protected by loved ones, and of feeling safe. My perception became that what I said and felt did not matter or was not accurate. I was unable to discern between what was really happening and what I thought was happening. Part of me felt wild and crazy. It was the beginning of having many health problems as well. Kidney, bladder, and throat infections, allergic reactions, heart problems, digestive disorders, nightmares, excessive fears, phobias, and depression colored much of the rest of my history. It was my beginning of grave insecurity with messages that darkness can never be trusted again, that good times can lead to the worst times. I feel it is significant to note that each trip I took after that tender age of three was an ordeal for me. I suffered from constipation because I refused to go to the bathroom, sometimes for up to five days. I ignored and denied all pressure and indications of pain until my tummy resembled that of a starving African with Kwashiorkor (severe malnutrition). Bloating or distention was a problem whenever I traveled, even into adulthood. It prevented me from enjoying vacations and from wanting to travel at all! It was as if everything stopped inside of me. Abdominal pain was my chief complaint even when at home, but trips were the worst.

After years of bits and pieces of memory coming back to me and of having professional therapy, I happened to be driving through Laramie, Wyoming. It was the summer of 1993 and something inside me said, "Well, now I have returned, and I am okay!" Great peacefulness filled my being. I felt strong and settled. While I know I can never prove what happened in that apartment that night, some things a person just knows to be true. The trauma of the sexual abuse felt truly resolved the day I drove through the city of Laramie feeling settled and strong.

The Tonsil Party

The third major trauma in my formative years began with my invitation to a 'tonsil party'. My sister and I were having frequent sore throats, and our doctor advised our parents to have our tonsils removed. Our dad was home for a few days from Wyoming, so they decided this would be an ideal time. It is important to keep in mind the prevailing philosophy at that time, in the late 1940s, was "the less you tell children, the better." The doctor advised my parents to tell us only that we were going to attend a tonsil party, with ice cream to boot! My parents did as he requested. Thus, I experienced an event that was portrayed as fun but was, in fact, very painful and distressing. My parents, who were supposed to love and protect, had lied to me. Whom could I trust? In my Mom's own words, "I have never forgotten those two brave, happy darlings walking down the hall with the nurse and my having to leave them. Yes, I cried, but they did not. I had second thoughts as I left the hospital."

The nurses assured us they would call our parents if we needed them, another promise that was broken throughout the night as I cried for Mommy. My uneasiness grew as they placed me in a crib (how insulting for a three-year-old) then took my temperature rectally. When they inserted the thermometer, I thought it was a knife. I believed my life was over, and indeed, it was threatened with a postoperative throat hemorrhage. I suffered pain and loneliness, along with frequent vomiting of blood. Knowing my sister was somewhere in a similar cubicle did not help my feelings of isolation. It is no wonder I literally almost died. I could not even swallow the ice cream they offered me. Nor could I swallow the craziness of my existence. The fight or flight survival mentality with its enduring resilience was keeping me alive, yet something within me had surrendered to a silent, unrelenting turmoil.

As recorded by my mother, "Louise recovered quickly, but Victoria didn't do well. The first night home her throat began to hemorrhage. All night I held her in my arms ready to rush her to the emergency room if the bleeding should increase–such a long frightening night for both of us. About 4:00 a.m. the bleeding stopped."

Three months passed, and Mom realized I had not bounced back since the surgery. "Victoria was no longer the happy, contented child I had been accustomed to. She was also running a slight fever. The doctor said I was just worrying too much, but I insisted on some tests, and they showed a definite increase in infection." Evidently, my entire tonsil had not been removed in the usual sac, and I had to have X-ray treatments for several weeks. The doctor put me on a very rigid schedule, because the heart muscle showed some damage similar to Rheumatic Fever. Mom says we played quieter games then, listened to more records, and read stories by the hour until I recovered.

I remember my mother's dedicated efforts to comfort and care for me. She made my favorite eggnog, played my treasured records, and slept next to me when I was nauseated. But nothing, it seemed, was ever enough to quiet the fear that was locked in my subconscious mind when I mistakenly assumed my Grandma's words, "Wilma will kill you if she finds out," were meant for me. The wedge it had placed between my mother and me would be unresolved for the next thirty-nine years.

II

DISCOVERY

"Open your eyes my dear."
"No, it might be too scary."
"Ah, but by keeping them closed, you feed the darker fears. The day will come when you will see and feel your hidden pain–and its discovery will direct your path to freedom and further light."

Victoria Lynn

Chapter 2

My Own Discovery of Abuse

People frequently ask the question, "Didn't you have previous clues that you had childhood sexual abuse in your background?" My reply is always "yes," followed by my explanation of a preschool presentation entitled, "The Touching Problem", that I attended in 1980.

The "Touching" Preschool Presentation

Parents and their four year olds filled our preschool meeting room, ready to view the educational program presented by local college student performers. There were three separate scenarios, each one depicting reactions of children who had been improperly touched.

I broke out in a sweat and at the program's conclusion had to go outside to get some fresh air. Upon returning to the group, I found it impossible to eat the refreshments. I knew something was very wrong. The inability to eat has always been my indicator that I am extremely upset! The child in me was all too familiar with what had been said that evening. The touching problem had been mine.

A Glimpse into Terror

Several years after the touching program, my confusing history surfaced again while riding in a car and casually talking with my sister about the recent silly styles of men's boxer shorts. I had a sudden image of a near nude man coming toward me. Profound anxiety caused me to feel like the walls of the car were compressing me, and I could not breathe. Although I was given hints of mistreatment, I was still unprepared for the return of the memory of my major CSA, which follows.

The Return

It is now important, yet extremely difficult, to share with you my very personal account of how my abuse experience returned to me. In order to open the chapter on discovery, I will move forward to the year 1987 and relate the trauma that occurred thirty-nine years after the initial offense.

The church parking lot, of all places. Right there in the church parking lot I sobbed, "I can't go in. No one likes me. I am bad!" My husband could not convince me otherwise. I felt I needed to be alone to cry. My husband indicated he would return to check on me, then went into the church. Neither of us realized my feelings of desperation would escalate to a dangerous degree. As I sat in the car, the confusion mounted. I was supposed to go to work right after my church meetings, and I was looking at that with a considerable amount of dread. The feeling of being out of control was devastating. The impulse to do something, anything, for relief prompted me to madly devour the lunch I had packed.

Somehow, I was able to drive home where I thought I might find comfort in the familiar refuge of the farmhouse I shared with my husband and six sons. Yet, upon arriving and throwing myself onto the bed, I had no awareness of familiar surroundings, or even of being a mother or a wife. I was feeling intense physical pain in the anal area and in my chest. I groped my way to the medicine cabinet where I knew there was leftover prescribed pain medication. As I writhed in pain from one side to another, my legs drawn upward and hugged to my chest, it was impossible for me to hold still or to think clearly. With such unrelenting physical pain and emotional upheaval, my only wish was to get relief, indeed to die for it. But, to my profound disappointment, death's release did not occur.

I remember screaming wildly, uttering words that made no sense. "Get out, get out. When the blood comes, I'll die." I recall thinking, "Why would I be repeating such absurdities and in such a strange, high-pitched voice?" I believed I had gone insane. At this point, the objectivity of my experience as a psychiatric nurse saved my sanity.

My desperation, the helplessness and hopelessness turned to curiosity as I tried to make sense out of what was happening. A sudden revelation came to me–these screams were those of a child who had been badly hurt, and they were released in a child's way of expressing anguish. Thus began my ascension out of terror. Shaking violently, I reached for the phone with the awareness I needed help now.

I called my family physician, and after describing my predicament, I blurted out, "Nothing relieves this intense physical pain!" His voice was reassuring, even though he explained there wasn't anything he could prescribe. This was a type of pain that needed to be felt in order to heal. He also said, "You are not the only woman who is going through this kind of experience." I cannot say I felt any of this information was helpful. The information was rational–I was not. He then gave me the name and number of a local therapist known for her empathy and extensive knowledge of abuse.

I believed the counselor would be shocked about what had just occurred. Nevertheless, I called and rattled off the details of the all-too-real nightmare. To my surprise, the counselor said, "How nice."

"How nice?" I stammered. "I'm scared out of my mind. I can hardly walk with this intense pain, and you're telling me this is nice?" I was astounded until she explained further, "How nice that little Victoria, who has been buried inside of you, finally felt safe enough to let you know what happened to her so long ago. You have hidden her terror inside you all these years, and you will know the secret. As an adult, you can help that part of you to feel safe, loved, and believed."

I slid down the wall into a crouched position, still holding the phone as the therapist continued, "I will see you in my office tomorrow, and we will work this through together. I am so pleased you had this breakthrough. It is not a breakdown. You will recover and be able to live a much fuller life now." I listened to every tender word given over the phone by a total stranger who understood. I felt so embarrassed talking about what had happened that I appreciated the anonymity of the phone. I came away from the two conversations feeling I was not so alone. It was comforting to hear there were others who also had been hurled back into their past and then thrust forward again.

The Options

Mother was curious as to why I would talk about what I believed happened to me as a child. After all, it was upsetting family members. My spontaneous reply to her was: "Mom, I felt I had three choices that day: 1) to die; 2) to go crazy; or 3) to tell. I chose the third."

The choice of the third option came from a process of elimination. I had already believed I was crazy, and I wanted to die. The only choice I had control over was to tell. Telling allowed me to live, and in living, I could question and research the mystery of what it all meant. I was able to think more of Little Victoria. I had listened to her cries; I believed her fearful state. I was determined to defend and protect her. With time I was able to validate her abuse with my grandmother's confession. (see page 103)

At some point, the unbearable pain relented. I felt compelled to verify the suspected abuse. With detective-like zeal and the help of others, I began to gather evidence. The one concept I could not grasp was the possibility of full recovery.

Chapter 3

Denial

A Close Look

While attending high school, my art teacher assigned us the intriguing task of enlarging a small item to fill an entire page in order to increase our ability to notice detail. I chose a walnut shell, spent hours drawing every ridge, and felt gratified in what I was learning from taking a close look at objects. I'm sure onlookers thought it strange that I would walk up to trees and almost touch them with my nose in order to study the details closely. This simple exercise taught me to pay close attention to my drawing. It also taught me to view many other things from a different perspective, allowing for a clearer picture. Walnuts remain a symbol to me of that great lesson.

Denial keeps us from taking a close look at our past, our present circumstances, and ourselves. It is known as a defense mechanism, is often unconscious, and can serve a useful function, especially for children with CSA. Denial is automatic and protective in that it allows the child to survive. The down side of denial is that it can also be costly, as it can prevent us from growing and moving on in our lives. Only when we can look squarely at a problem and admit it really exists can we begin to evaluate and modify it.

Increased Awareness

The Battle of the Bulge

As we were eating our breakfast one morning, the children and I heard a drip, drip sound coming from a little bulge in the ceiling. We had noticed the bulge months earlier, but we believed the problem had been corrected. Not so. In order to determine if it was wet or not, I put my finger into it. Whoops! We now had a hole in the ceiling and roof that would require considerable repair. We could have fixed it months earlier when it was just barely a little discoloration and saved a lot of money and hard work.

I use this analogy to demonstrate how I learned that addressing the past as it resurfaced increased my confidence in my ability to respond more quickly to each of 'the bulges' that presented themselves. It was interesting to discover that my body and mind had marvelous ways to give me clues as to when I needed assistance. I had to learn to be willing to experiment with my responses and methods of support in order to become more secure in my own being. Past personal experience suggests that perhaps too many women are tempted to wait until their symptoms become potentially dangerous before taking a good look at the reality of the situation. They may live their lives in quiet desperation, never getting so symptomatic that they have a nervous breakdown. They may or may not be suicidal. They tend to resign themselves to the idea of unhappiness as their lot in life.

A Look at the Past

A friend of mine chooses to avoid looking at her past. She says she keeps it behind her head so even if she turns her head, she cannot see it. The problem is it takes energy to keep it there. She cannot learn from it, nor can she see the good parts of her past. It appears to me that when we have a need to obscure bad memories, the side effect is that good memories are also blocked. The brain does not seem capable of discerning which is which, especially for children. This could be one explanation why many adults who were abused as children cannot remember much of their childhood.

Another friend of mine insisted he did not want to deal with his past, which involved a crippling accident. He was aware of his past, yet his decision to not deal with it seemed to give his history great power over him. One day, using a NLP strategy, (see Resources) I respectfully asked him if he would like to put his past into a thick walled plastic tube to his side. We then pretended to attach it to him with only a thin string. Now, he could look at it whenever he chose in order to obtain useful information. More important, he liked the control of this simple method of selectively looking and learning.

Puzzling Pieces

Anyone who has ever put a five-hundred-piece puzzle together wonders in the back of his/her mind if there is going to be a missing piece. It is so disappointing at the end to find the dog did eat one piece, or that it got vacuumed up, or the manufacturer did not put all the pieces in the box. We do family puzzles over the Thanksgiving and Christmas holidays, and it is always a great relief if all the pieces are there. We sit back, look at the puzzle, and say, "We did it!" Then we can put the puzzle away.

When I was working on my personal abuse puzzle, I was frustrated because I could not find all the pieces. Some pieces did not seem to fit. I tried so hard to get the entire abuse picture to come back to me all at once. "Let the whole picture come together. Then I can put the lid on the box and put it away on a shelf!" But, it just didn't work that way. Not being able to see the whole picture together, made it more frightening and left me feeling even more out of control.

It was difficult to accept the process of discovery and recovery. It was far more productive for me to acknowledge that perhaps for my own protection, the puzzle was delayed and may never be complete. I had not felt ready to receive the first major abuse piece, but at least I was older, more experienced and had a much greater repertoire of coping abilities than I did as a child. Most certainly, I felt like I would die with nearly every revealed memory. I did not die; I survived. I choose to believe the Lord allowed me to work through fragments, as I was able to handle them.

I had a choice. I could choose to be angry, distressed and fearful, or to worry constantly about the memories, when they were going to come, and what would be the outcome of their return. I chose to allow the memories to come when they would, and if at any time it seemed to be more than I could bear, I learned to say, "That is enough for now." With practice, I became adept enough to mentally put the abuse puzzle into a box, put the box on the shelf, and leave it there until I needed to reopen it in order to deal with another piece.

Chapter 4

Flashback,
"Step Forward"

While attending a national convention of VOICES, Victims of Incest Can Emerge Survivors (see Resources), Laurieann Chutis, taught a number of us interested in leading incest survival support groups. As a social worker, she shared material that has been most useful in my own treatment, as well as for helping others. With her permission, I am including a portion of her information on flashbacks:

> *Flashbacks are memories of past traumas. They may take the form of pictures, sounds, smells, body sensations, feelings, or the lack of them (numbness). Many times, there is no actual visual or auditory memory. One may have the sense of panic, being trapped, feeling powerless with no memory stimulating it. These experiences can also happen in dreams.*
>
> *As children (or adolescents), we had to insulate ourselves from the emotional and physical horrors of trauma. In order to survive, that insulated child remained isolated, unable to express the feelings and thoughts of that time. It is as though we put that part into a time capsule until it full blown in the present comes out*
>
> *When that part comes out, the little one is experiencing the past as if it were happening today. As the flashback occurs, it is as if we forget that we have an adult part available to us for reassurance, protection and grounding. The intense feelings and body sensations occurring are so frightening because the feelings/sensations are not related to the reality of the present and many times seem to come from out of nowhere.*
>
> *We begin to think we are crazy and are afraid of telling*

*anyone (including our therapist) of these experiences. We feel
out of control and at the mercy of our experiences. We begin to
avoid situations and stimuli that we think triggered it. Many
times flashbacks occur during any form of sexual intimacy, or
a trigger may be a person who has similar characteristics as
the perpetrator, or it may be a situation today that stirs up
similar trapped feelings (confrontation, aggressive people).*

*If you are feeling young, and if you are experiencing
stronger feelings than are called for in the present situation,
you are experiencing a flashback.*

The above information gave me something with which to connect
my experience. The incident in the church parking lot jolted me out
of denial, and now I could give it an identity–flashback. With the
accompanying physical pain, my body, spirit and emotions
dramatically forced me into realizing I was reliving a previous
trauma.

I am aware there are those who give no credence to the concept of
flashbacks or repressed memory. For me, it helps to identify and
categorize the experience. Calling it a flashback fits–it is a piece of
the past hitting like a bolt of lightning. Readers are free to label such
an experience any way they choose, but calling it something has been
important to my healing process.

Flashback support

LaurieAnn Chutis also offers some specific helps for dealing with
flashbacks that I found particularly useful:

- Tell yourself that you are having a flashback
- Remind yourself that the worst is over. The feelings and
  sensations you are experiencing are memories of the past. The
  actual event took place long ago when you were little and you
  survived. Now it is time to let out that terror, rage, hurt, and/or
  panic. Now is the time to honor your experience.
- Get grounded. This means stamping your feet on the ground so
  that the little one knows you have feet and can get away now if
  you need to. (As a child, you couldn't get away; now you can.)

- Breathe. When we are really frightened, we stop normal breathing. As a result, our body begins to panic from the lack of oxygen. Lack of oxygen in itself causes a great many panic feelings: pounding in the head, tightness, sweating, feeling faint, shakiness and dizziness. When we breathe deeply enough, much of the panic feeling can decrease. Breathing deeply means putting your hand on your diaphragm and breathing deeply enough so that your diaphragm pushes against your hand, and then exhaling so that the diaphragm goes in.
- Re-orient to the present. Begin to use your five senses in the present. Look around and see the colors in the room, the shapes of things, the people nearby, etc. Listen to the sounds in the room–your breathing, traffic, birds, people, cars, etc. Feel your body and what is touching it; your clothes, your own arms and hands, the chair or floor supporting you.
- Speak to the little one inside and reassure her/him. It is very healing to get your adult in the picture so your little one now knows safety.
- Get in touch with your need for boundaries. Sometimes when we are having a flashback we lose the sense of where we leave off and the world begins, as if we do not have skin. Wrap yourself in a blanket, hold a pillow or stuffed animal, go to bed, sit in a closet–any way that you can feel yourself truly protected from the outside.
- Get support. Depending on your situation, you may need to be alone or may want someone near you. In either case, it is important that your close ones know about flashbacks so they can help you with the process, whether that means letting you be by yourself or being there with you.
- Take time to recover. Sometimes flashbacks are very powerful. Give yourself the time to make the transition from this powerful experience. Do not expect yourself to jump into adult activities right away. Take a nap or a warm bath, or enjoy some quiet time. Be kind and gentle with yourself. Do not beat yourself up for having a flashback. Appreciate how much your little one went through as a child.
- Honor your experience. Appreciate yourself for having survived that horrible time as a child. Respect your body's need to experience those feelings of long ago.

- Be patient. It takes time to heal the past. It takes time to learn appropriate ways of taking care of self, of being an adult who has feelings, and developing effective ways of coping in the here and now.
- Find a competent therapist. Look for one who understands the processes of healing from incest. A therapist can be a guide, a support and a coach in this healing process. You do not have to do it alone . . . ever again.
- Join a self-help group. Survivors are wonderful allies in this process of healing. It is a healing thing to share your process with others who understand so deeply what you are going through.

It makes sense that a flashback represents age regression with intrusive memories of the traumatic experience trying to surface in order to be healed. Know that you are not crazy; you are healing. For those of us who have suffered horrendous flashbacks accompanied with pain, confirmation of our abuse is given. As bizarre and extreme as my initial discovery was, it worked for me as nothing else could. I know what I know. For me, my grandmother's devastating confession, which came months after my initial major flashback, would be vital–I would have a witness. Yet, even without her words, I would know what I know. My body and spirit have confirmed to me the validity of my own abuse. If I were to deny it, I would be lying and untrue to my core self.

Flashbacks Can Be Useful

A question I frequently hear is: "How can having frightening flashbacks be considered in any way positive?" My response is that flashbacks often provide needed clues to personal abuse otherwise left unrecognized, and thus, untreated. Secondly, the time-release capsule continues to present a challenge to survivors–the challenge of facing fear. I found overcoming fear and dread is a learned skill that has strengthened me personally. Flashbacks have provided multiple opportunities for me to condition myself to wellness.

Addressing the flashbacks as they came increased my confidence in my ability to face each succeeding flashback. As I did my recovery work, the flashbacks seem to taper off. Somewhere along the line, I determined if I am to have these uninvited terror trips dropping in on me, then I had better really enjoy the times in between. I made this decision about six years ago while standing in our garage following a full-blown flashback. That very day I began to squeeze every possible bit of joy from life in order to make each day worth living.

My Silent Struggle

Moreover, there I stand as if dropped from another time into a familiar setting, now unfamiliar, without defense, and terror ridden, until at last I stamp my feet upon solid ground and declare, "This is now, and I have grown!"

Flashbacks may give us clues to our abuse history, but often they do not make any sense. They just happen and at times when they are most unwanted. I will share with you one that occurred at my mother's home. The house was brimming with company and preparations for my grandmother's funeral, which was to be held on the following day. My sister and I had rehearsed the song we were planning to perform at the funeral, and for some reason my voice was lacking in volume, tone and quality. Mother even commented on it. I felt her strong disapproval and the flashback enveloped me.

I could not speak. I was aware of others around me, but I felt totally helpless. No one else was aware of my intense suffering. I headed for the guest room where I took a tranquilizer from my purse. (I had learned there is a time and a place for medication, and this was the time and place! I was still dependent upon the occasional use of the tranquilizers, which my doctor had recommended I use until I became desensitized.) The company was calling to me that we would be leaving for the family dinner in fifteen minutes. Although deeply troubled, a large part of me did not want to miss the dinner. In addition, I did not want to be the sick daughter I had been during much of my life.

For solace, while awaiting the medication's relief, I tried to read some comforting quotes I carry with me. I could not read. I was later impressed with the probability that I was too young at that moment to know how to read. It was as if I had briefly reverted to age three. The words were meaningless letters. Still shaken from the episode, it took a great deal of courage, combined with hunger and curiosity, for me to enter the vehicle waiting to take us to the restaurant. I chalked the event up to experience and marveled at the struggle I had silently endured.

Flashbacks need to be recognized and understood as much as possible. They are an effective way for our mind and body to release toxic material that interferes with our growth. Although they hold life and death potential, they are treatable. A full life can be lived in spite of them. When you have a flashback, identify it as such. Then step forward and appreciate the opportunity to deal with an emotional state from the past. You can be your best reassurance. As unpleasant as flashbacks are, they get our full attention and can lead us to eventual understanding, acceptance and peace.

III

TROUBLESOME AFTER EFFECTS

Our society concerns itself over the possible detrimental side effects of medications. I maintain that the side effects (or after effects) of childhood sexual abuse are also potentially toxic, and therefore deserving of recognition and effective treatment in an effort to reduce human suffering.

Victoria Lynn

Chapter 5

Adolescent After Effects

As a child, I thought I functioned quite well. As an adult who has put the puzzle together, I recognize that my physical body exhibited the symptoms my mind could not express. From the age of four to thirteen, I was energetic, had many friends, and was a favored student with high scholastic ability. However, I was a nail biter (a symptom of deep seated anxiety) and suffered from stomachaches, frequent bouts of other illnesses, and occasional nightmares; otherwise, the interim years were remarkably unremarkable.

Then I reached my teenage years. Most of us are aware of the various trials faced by teenagers during the critical years of adolescence; however, it's apparent to me that my challenges extended beyond the norm as I entered into a world of frightening despair. The following examples taken from my worst teenage year are sad, yet enlightening. They illustrate some of the disabling effects of a history of childhood sexual abuse when combined with hormonal changes. Eruptions of hysteria, panic attacks, and severe depression were overwhelming and resulted in my release from attending school for over eight months. I remember feeling crazy at times and in great physical distress. Even today, my stomach sickens a bit when I go back in my mind to that difficult thirteenth year.

School Phobia

Returning to its foreboding entrance
Was as returning to flames of fire
So intense . . . my fear of school.

As a thirteen-year-old traveling with my mom in our car toward the dreaded appointment with the psychiatrist, my outlook was bleak. "Am I crazy? Oh, please, Lord, don't let this happen to me." The dreary November weather mirrored my sense of gloom and doom. "I'll never lie down on a couch. I'll die first." And the pain in my abdomen seemed to verify that possibility because its intensity caused me to double over as I rode in the back seat of the family car. The medical doctors had determined the pain was all in my head, but it certainly felt like it was all in my stomach.

Surprisingly, the doctor spent most of his time with my mother, while I hid in the bathroom of the waiting area. Once I was coaxed from the bathroom into his office, the doctor's only advice to me was to draw and then to bring my pictures along to each appointment–no tears, no couch, no fancy talk. The psychiatrist agreed with the family physician that I had somatic illness. He explained that my school phobia was a separation anxiety reaction caused by being away from my mother. However, even when with her, I did not feel at ease. I spent long afternoons with my mother, who worked in a local beauty shop. Occasionally, I passed the days quietly with grandmas and endured even longer days at home alone.

Months passed slowly and the thoughts of returning to school were still terrifying. No one had the heart or the ability to force me to go to school. I spent my lengthy timeout being tutored, playing the piano, drawing, painting and wondering what was going to become of me. Since I was such a nervous child, my mother suggested that my piano teacher give me only simple pieces–nothing too challenging or stressful.

The only safe place seemed to be in my own bedroom, where I was able to isolate and insulate myself from additional pressures. I remember feeling like such a weirdo. My friends were told only that I had a nutritional deficiency that required vitamin shots. Even with regular visits and encouragement from my best girl friend, I seldom left my room.

The psychiatrist also explained to my parents that there was a psychological conflict between my unusually small stature (that of a fifth grader) and an extremely bright intellect (that of a high school age student). It was a relief to me simply to know the doctor did not think I was crazy.

I remember times when I resented having missed that year of school, when I wished I could have dealt with the fears more quickly.

However, my time-out could be interpreted as a much-needed break from stressors that were beyond my coping abilities at that crucial time in my life.

My mother shared some of her original dread of taking me to a psychiatrist. She simply had run out of ideas on how to help her underweight daughter, who seemed to be pining away–no longer taking interest in her usual activities. Mother was aware I had attempted to be like the other students, and that I was certainly bright, yet the migraine headaches had developed, and the stomachaches made it impossible for me to sit through classes. I would often call to be picked up from school, and then wait outside the building for her arrival. My fear of returning inside was so intense–as if the building were on fire. My mother had dutifully taken me to various family doctors, seeking the causes for my physical distress. It was difficult to follow the psychiatrist's suggestion that she stop taking me to work with her. I appeared to be so unhappy that leaving me home alone seemed negligent somehow, yet she complied. The school phobia was another reminder to my distraught mother that "something was wrong with Victoria."

Reading the *Anxiety and Phobia Workbook*, by Edmund J. Bourne, helped me to understand that simple phobias typically involve a strong fear and avoidance of one particular type of object or situation. My phobia was far from simple, as there were panic attacks, agoraphobia (fear of having a panic attack in a situation without help available) and fear of humiliation/embarrassment in social situations.

Obsessive Compulsiveness

Now everything is under control–as long as
Everything is under my control.
With every detail just so . . .
Dare not to rearrange
The patterns of my living.
For in them lie
My only grasp
Of sanity.

Though my mother taught me to be orderly, I was an extremist.

My top desk drawer in my bedroom was an example of compulsive orderliness. Every box containing items such as paper clips, elastics and staples fit perfectly together, having been arranged and maintained just so. In addition, I labeled the clear plastic containers with exactness for identification.

What my mother did not know was each night I was driven to obsessively count the pennies that filled the blue bank resting on my dresser. Other daily rituals included jumping rope one hundred times and playing imaginary hopscotch on the pillow with my fingers until I fell asleep. I had adapted to my frequent bouts of nausea by yawning again and again. Focusing on the repetitions brought relief. I felt compelled to go to bed at precisely ten o'clock each night. I expected the rest of the family to go to bed then also, because noise kept me awake. I dreaded any "no activity" time because that meant an opportunity to think and to feel. I could not bear the resulting distress. Patterns of sameness, ritual and strangely enough, *sickness* were my areas of perceived safety. I had nowhere else to go.

I recovered from my phobias, and the time-consuming obsessive rituals subsided; yet I remained compulsively neat. I often tended for a neighbor, a mother of five, with whom I identified because she also liked everything in perfect order. When the woman died suddenly, maintaining such perfection no longer appealed to me, and I surrendered my compulsive orderliness to the cluttered room of a typical teenager. My mother's once-grave concern for my need for perfect control shifted to the minor irritations of my messy bedroom.

Eating Disorder

> *Sometimes life was just plain hard to stomach*
> *And nourishing my body would have meant surrender*
> *To its confusing demands for survival.*

Food never really interested me. Small of stature, weighing less than 80 pounds, I could ill afford weight loss at this time in my life when I needed to grow and develop. Although everyone else appreciated my mother's excellent cooking, I had no interest in food. Indeed, at times when I felt extremely anxious, all food smelled and tasted similar. The horrible blandness often sent me crying to my room. Then, too, eating usually meant more stomachaches. Certain odors also caused flashbacks. With intense nausea, I often felt like inducing vomiting but usually resisted the temptation. White rice with butter, donuts, and Ovaltine were my mainstays.

I did not have the full-blown condition of anorexia nervosa, which has received much attention in recent years. I did not have a distorted body image, nor was I trying to be thinner, but I was anorexic in that I had very little appetite or desire to eat. I believe the lack of appetite went along with the depression (another side effect of CSA). It is also possible I used it as a way to say "no" to mother's understandable attempts to have me eat.

Twelve years ago, I attended a community class provided by our local hospital on the topic of Eating Disorders (ED). The presenting doctor claimed that 90 percent (or more in his opinion) of those suffering from an ED have a history of sexual abuse. Following the lecture, I talked with him and shared my unforgettable, one and only bulimic experience after the flashback in the church parking lot.

Nightmares

Asleep.
Release, at last
From conscious thoughts

Yet haunted still
With fear-formed dreams
My sleep remained a risk.

Awake.
And daylight too
Unfairly brought
Some dreams of fear.
Within the safety of my room
The monster entered in.

Nightmares haunted me day and night. Often, I would hear house creaks that I interpreted as invaders upstairs when no one else was home. On one occasion, I screamed to my mother that there was a man under my bed. Of course it was not so, but to me it was such a real image of a man entering my bedroom and then hiding under the bed that I could not be comforted.

Typical nightmares consisted of scenes of fires burning out of control within my neighborhood, engulfing my home, and then forcing me to the edge of a nearby gully. Even as a child, the fire scene from The Wizard of Oz caused me to hide behind the theater seats. It was years before I dared to watch the scene again to see for myself that the fiery Oz's appearance was merely the Wizard's creation.

During the fearful time of my thirteenth year, I was home alone watching a film of the Hindenberg, the blimp that burst into flames over New York City in 1937. With my excessive inner terror, I had no tolerance for further fright. I panicked, running upstairs, unable to free myself from the horror I had just witnessed on the TV screen. I remember feeling angry that the film had caught me off guard. The incident caused me to increase my vigilance by avoiding newspapers and by carefully monitoring my exposure to television.

To my great relief, the nightmares subsided as I matured. I made peace with the night as I faced my worst fears. Yet, caring for burn victims was my most difficult nursing assignment. When asked to assist physicians with a new admit, a young boy who had been trapped in a car fire, I quickly had to enter the utility closet nearby and pray mightily for the courage to help.

I rarely suffer with nightmares today. Most of my dreams are insightful, colorful communications I enjoy before fully awakening.

Successful Return to School

The other students
did not see me.

For I was hidden
within the car
behind the trees.

While drawing their school–
my school.

But I saw them
  as they drew me
    back into their midst.

By the end of my thirteenth year the school phobia, agoraphobia, and social phobia were resolved. The psychiatrist's final drawing assignment for me to draw my junior high school was my most productive.

My stepfather coerced me into driving with him to the school one morning for this purpose. We sat unnoticed in the little car parked behind some trees on the road in front of the previously dreaded school building. As I drew my picture I was so envious of the other students as they sauntered up to the school and entered without a problem. It was then that my desire to return overpowered my fears, and I successfully attended the last week of the seventh grade. I wonder if without treatment, I would have remained hiding in my bedroom. Three cheers for a doctor's art therapy, for a determined family and for a victorious young lady who survived a challenging school year!

Chapter 6

Somatic Illness

In a class I attended on alcoholism, the instructor informed us that persons with a history of CSA commonly have two disorders:

- Addiction - Included were addictions to drugs, alcohol, sex, painful abusive relationships and eating disorders.

- Somatic illness - Somatic illness is a disorder characterized by recurrent multiple physical complaints and symptoms for which there is no organic cause.[1] The symptoms are not under voluntary control and, as we are realizing, they can contribute to actual disease. The symptoms have a so-called, hysterical element, and the suffering person often seeks the advice of many doctors.[2]

I did not like to fall into either category, so I told myself that I am the exception, having none of the above symptoms. But I was somewhat intrigued by the second disorder, somatic illness. I had to admit that pain had been a theme for most of my life. It was, in fact, my reality. I figured out, even as a small child, that my body always hurt somewhere, primarily in the stomach. There was a time when illness was my personal retreat, an almost welcomed break from daily patterns, a familiar place of indulgence and rest. That is, until I had to face a chronic, perplexing and life threatening condition.

Somatic or Not?

It Only Happened Once
After the flashback in 1987, I had several incredibly healthy, energetic months. I became an avid race walker, rounding the high

school track each morning with great vitality and fitness. The results of a devastating conversation with my grandmother ended that brief period of wellness and led my doctors and me on a confusing, life-saving race.

I don't remember Grandma ever yelling at me before, but in a phone conversation the initial disclosure of my sexual abuse unnerved her. She told me I was wrong to tell of my "supposed" abuse. I responded defensively by blurting out my feelings. She kept saying, "No, no, don't say such things." Finally, she exclaimed, "It only happened once, and it was not your father!" I wrote her words on a piece of paper. I then begged her to tell me who it was that abused me. She was silent. I held the paper as evidence, but the price of the confession was the loss of my lifeline. Grandma was no longer there for me. That night I collapsed onto our couch and spent the entire night curled up tightly with clenched fists. The next morning I felt too weak to exercise, and when I did return to the track, my coordination was off. I felt light headed, and worst of all, only my left side experienced the sensation of being cold; the right side was almost completely numb.

Cries for Help

At various times in my life, I experienced the agony of constant worry about symptoms, from first awakening in the morning until my final, fearful thought before falling asleep. However, I explained to my family physician that the torment had never been this troublesome. He was aware of CSA dynamics and attempted to be objective after his examination, which did indicate my right side had less sensation. I feared I had multiple sclerosis, a brain tumor, or a psychosomatic condition–the conversion hysteria type. After all, the symptoms developed after my devastating conversation with my grandmother. I willingly sought a psychiatrist who agreed I had some conversion hysteria symptoms: impaired coordination or balance, localized weakness, loss of touch sensation, and episodes of paralysis. He also looked at the MRI results that diagnosed a physical condition of ACM (Arnold Chiari Malformation of the brain stem). Several consulting physicians felt my physical complaints were in excess of what they would expect from the test results. It took the insistence of a neurologist and neurosurgeon to explain how they could attribute all of my symptoms to the herniated brain stem and pressure on the spinal cord. Only major surgery would relieve the pressure.

My research on the ACM surgical outcome was not positive: 50/50 chance of some improvement, yet most patients continued to have neurological problems following surgery. My symptoms seemed too extreme for the small amount of herniation, but still they worsened. Walking was difficult, even with my legs spread 18 inches apart for balance; I could not judge distance and had to surrender driving privileges. I had bouts of temporary paralysis of my right leg, increased headaches, and inability to see well caused from nystagmus (eye tremors). Tranquilizers and antidepressants were helpful. Although I was not suicidal, my will to live under such devastating conditions was waning.

Proof at Last

The critical juncture in the decision making process was when I lost my gag reflex and began to choke on food and water. I was told my respirations would go next. My condition, left untreated, would be fatal. The neurosurgeon called me at my home to say he felt he could help me, but I needed a stronger will to live or he would not dare operate. He asked me to trust him. The psychiatrist was consulted, and he affirmed his belief that I had enough spunk to live, even as a handicapped person. The decision was made to operate.

A prayer meeting was held for my support before the surgery. My son called the meeting a "living funeral" because we sang a hymn and had speakers. An inspired religious leader told me I would live to see my grandchildren. That hope, combined with the faith and prayers of many, strengthened me.

The surgery was successful, and although I had two postoperative brushes with death, I lived, was able to walk straight, and to see well again. I learned, unbeknown to the doctors and to me, a cyst had enlarged to the point of causing the exaggerated symptoms. If I had not had the surgery, I would have died.

Survival Again

In retrospect, I can see the extra dimension that my abuse history added to my illness. It complicated matters and confused the focus. The emotional factors almost prevented me from getting the surgical relief from the pressure:

- It is dangerous to assume that symptoms that often accompany a history of CSA are, by themselves, of an emotional nature.
- It is also incorrect to assume that having such symptoms is proof positive that one has a background of CSA.
- It is my responsibility to work with any symptoms that reduce my effectiveness and ability to live an active life with a degree of joyfulness.
- With my grandmother's rejection, an area of weakness gave way to debilitating symptoms that, if left untreated, would have led to my death.

It was necessary to survive the effects of CSA more than once following the initial abuse: Re-experiencing the abuse as an adult, via the memories, the illness following the disclosure, and now, the collapse following the surgery.

"And When You Are Ready"

I was feeling envious as I watched the lecturer walk effortlessly across the floor. He was on stage, pain free and relaxed. I was the observer, plagued with tightened neck and shoulder muscles, limited motion, growing impatience, and a longing for relief.

"The day might come when you (speaking to his audience) will let go of the headaches, neck and back pain. The day just might come when you're ready."

I am sure I was glaring at the speaker as I thought: "Sounds easy for you. Well, it seems I have already tried everything, and my pain continues–poor me, the exception. Yet, it would be liberating. Can I even remember what it was like to feel consistently well? If the day might come, how do I get ready for it? I don't know . . . maybe I'd better not get my hopes up."

Surgery to relieve pressure in my skull and neck had been successful in that I could walk well, judge distances, and had more feeling restored to my limbs. Yet, it seemed my incision would not heal entirely. Even very limited motion hurt. I spent hours lying uncomfortably in bed. My headaches increased and my hands burned unbearably at times (a condition known as neuropathy). The crippling of spirit and body continued.

Reaching Out

The Call

A furnace inspector suggested there might be a crack in our furnace causing deadly carbon monoxide to leak into our home. When he mentioned the symptoms caused by its fumes we realized that, indeed, we had experienced some nausea and extraordinary feelings of fatigue, especially when we were in the basement room next to the furnace. He told us to call the gas company, whose representative said they would send a worker out within the hour. In the meantime, a close inspection of the furnace revealed no cracks anywhere. When the carbon monoxide meter registered no detectable amount, I again called the gas company to tell them it would not be necessary to send anyone over. However, the company representative would not take no for an answer. In fact, by law they had to come once called. I thought, "I've over reacted, and now I feel ridiculous." As it turned out, it was a very god thing the gas company did follow through. The man who came one hour later found wind had been forcing insidious toxic fumes into our basement that were poisoning us and our home. How many of us hesitate to call for help, fearing that our alarm may not be justified?

Seeking Assistance

One day I exploded. I kicked the cupboards and screamed, "I'm sick of hurting, sick of too much pain, sick of being helpless, sick of big people (where did that one come from?), sick of feeling naked (another surprise)!" I grabbed the telephone book in final desperation and called every service I could think of, including the local pain clinic, my family doctor, a new neurologist in town, social services, a hypnotherapist, the local hospital, a friend, and a church leader. It was time. Time to discover the truth. Am I to be disabled for life? Can I recover from the effects of brain surgery, now five years past? How serious is this malformation of the brain stem? Do I have fibromyalgia (a form of painful arthritis)? Is all this pain psycho-somatic (emotionally based)? I had once again opened the book to take a good look with some professionals at pages that might have been missed, to see why the chapters on pain kept repeating themselves.

The underlying question was, "What is wrong with me?" During my childhood, "What's wrong with you, Victoria?" was the question asked, not only by me, but also by others. The implications of the query took my thoughts down many frightening paths. The unspoken message seemed to be: "We're weary of your illnesses and unhappiness; there is nothing really wrong with you; Get over it; Stop exaggerating; Maybe you are crazy!"

After making appointments with several people trained to detect health problems and to assist in their resolution, I felt ridiculous. I wanted out of my commitment and to relieve them of theirs. It was so humiliating to admit my misery, and I determined I would not color the picture with my background because they would think it was somatic illness for sure. Soon my phone was ringing with appointments, insurance approvals, expectations, and reassurances. The ball was rolling. I wanted to call it all off by claiming, "False alarm, folks. I'll be fine."

There was a lesson to learn from both stories. Some conditions cannot be recognized or corrected alone, no matter how insightful, knowledgeable or willing we are. I learned there are times when people need others who have expertise beyond their own.

Helpful Hope from "The Secret Garden"

People at the local pain clinic recognized I was in unbearable pain as I watched my biofeedback reading remain active no matter how hard I tried to relax. I sat there and cried. During the exam by the physician, I sensed his discouragement, perhaps reflecting my own. The clinic had recently treated two other women with the same ACM diagnosis, so they were aware of the complications. He told me the clinic did not produce miracles, that he had never seen a miracle, and the best he could predict would be an increase of one hour in my activity each day. The director was much more positive and said they would help me get back to work. Through no fault of the examiners, the exams, which included squeezing fingers and lifting my arms against opposition, further injured my neck. Ironically, the following day I was in too much pain to return to the pain clinic. The staff was supportive, and the tender physical therapist almost cried with me in empathy. They admitted I would suffer even more pain in doing exercises and that further evaluation by a neurologist would be a good choice.

When my condition was at its peak and I was confined to my bed, the greater part of each day with unrelenting neck and shock-like hand pain, muscle spasms, and mounting anxiety, I was desperate for hope. The electrifying pain of irritated nerves unnerved me. A neurosurgeon admitted that sometimes after this type of surgery involving skull segment removal and neck fusion, these symptoms simply do occur. He kept defending the brain surgeon, as if he suspected I was going to sue him, saying, "You needed the operation. It saved your life!" He almost yelled as he insisted, "There is nothing else that can be done!"

I left his office, hating doctors, medicine, nerves, men, cars, traffic, having to climb the stairs, and my tiresome bed to which I returned. I felt hopeless.

Since holding a book up to read was uncomfortable, I discovered that listening to an audio book read on tape would fill the void. I listened to *The Secret Garden*, by Francis Burnett, a touching story of a child who believed he was deformed, and then later discovered that his problem was his own perception of his condition. His houseguest beguiled him into a world beyond his suffering, the secret garden. He was given the challenge of accepting the thrill of hope or of continuing in his imprisonment of illness. He dared to look at himself, to breathe fresh air, to plot and play with children, and even to desert his wheelchair.

Hope is a powerful concept. The lack of it brings despair. As a nurse, I thought, if hope were measurable, say in a blood test, it could be determined when a person is in serious need of a transfusion. Perhaps it was this, or similar thoughts, that infused me with renewed hope. Ideas came: mild exercise in a warm shower, restricted use of my hands for several weeks, additional therapy, and securing funds for treatment. Maybe somehow I could heal enough to help others. With that sincere desire, wanting to touch other's lives for the better, the door opened, and I ventured out into the garden.

"Can't Is Not in My Vocabulary"

The new neurologist in town greeted me warmly. Having cried most of the morning, I was at my worst when he saw me. It was helpful, actually, because my defenses and pretenses were spent. He listened to my woeful tale and began the task of my recovery, later admitting to me his belief that "If I can cure Victoria, I can cure anyone." I immediately became his challenge and he ordered numerous tests. "You must do what I say to get well. I want you to take this medication every night."

"Oh great," I thought, "an antidepressant. He thinks I'm depressed, and I'm not." The doctor explained that my depression was justifiable and well masked. He said the medication would allow the nerve endings to rest and heal during the night, as well as in the day–and that a continual dose of its mild muscle relaxant component would greatly decrease my pain and limited movements. I was admonished to be more active and to resume my walking exercise to which I responded, "but I can't."

"Can't is not in my vocabulary," he stressed. "I am from the Korean Resistance. If I had used the word *can't,* I would be dead today. Even with your history of abuse, you can recover."

I had met my match. I took the drug faithfully. I had not felt such marvelous relaxation since my visit to the Center for InnerChange in Denver. I had been too proud to consider using an antidepressant, nor would I admit how depressed I had become. Why did I believe I could have chronic pain for all those months without depression?

After completing many tests, and compiling old records, I had my second appointment with the neurologist. He told me, "In the past you have been working hard but going in the wrong direction." I had been trying to heal by taking it easy, doing as little as possible, protecting my painful neck and regularly re-injuring it by reaching, sleeping wrong, even by becoming tense. He explained it might take six months to a year, but I could recover 90 percent of my ability to function, to move and perhaps to have less painful hands. I felt as ignorant as a little child being taught the very basics of treatment. The treatment for my chronic pain syndrome would include medication, massage and physical therapy. He handed me a sheet describing basic stretches I was to do three times each day.

"That's it?" I questioned.

"Listen to your body," he instructed. "Do not overdo. Call me day or night if you have increased pain. I will always be there for you. This is the way I work. Tell the insurance company you have 10 kinds of pain: physical, emotional, cultural, and more. You have chronic pain syndrome resulting from surgery and the ACM. You are intelligent. You will recover." Within nine months I was able to work again, and the hand pain was greatly reduced. I was off all medication one year later.

Now my concept of pain is altered. It is part of my human experience, and I am neither immune from it nor expecting more than others. I have developed greater compassion for others who experience chronic pain and can truly relate to them with empathy. Pain seems to be a common denominator. But, having a greater understanding of it does not mean I have to experience it continually. The tendency to slip into somatization (the changing of mental experiences or states into physical symptoms) remains a challenge. I accept the fact that symptoms are my body's method of communicating with me, and my task is to be an interpreter. I also believe that symptoms are often the result of buried feelings. The reader may be interested in the extensive list of "Probable Feelings Causing Illness" in Karol Truman's Book, *Feelings Buried Alive Never Die.* With Karol's permission, I'll share the following from her book:

> *What you may not realize is that when negative feelings are not resolved as they occur, these feelings remain very much alive in your physical energy field (body) and these feelings affect each day of your life.*
>
> *Somehow, somewhere, in some aspect of your life the effect of these negative feelings WILL be realized. They will make themselves known when you least expect it. These buried feelings may suddenly, after smoldering or fermenting for who knows how long—become apparent in your physical well-being. How? One way is through dis-ease. . . . Feelings that we have buried and are completely unaware of are what create the challenges, the uneasiness, the dis-ease, the pain and the crises situations in our lives.*[3]

Learning to release negative feelings using the book's specific suggestions has been an effective method of healing for me.

I have realized that it is important for physical and mental health to seek help. In so doing, I also learned it is imperative that I be honest with treatment providers and with myself. It was not something I wanted to do. However, even as a nurse, it came as a surprise to me that my background does affect my overall diagnoses and treatment. I now keep in mind, "And when you're ready...."

Notes

1. *Mosby's Medical Nursing and Allied Health Dictionary*,5th Edition
2.DSM IV, *Diagnostic and Statistical Manual of Mental Disorders*, American Psychiatric Association, 1998.)
3. Karol K. Truman, *Feelings Buried Alive Never Die*...(Las Vegas, Nevada,1991), pp. 2,3.

Chapter 7

Triggers to Childhood Sexual Abuse Memories

Certain situations, places, or persons may trigger memories of the original sexual abuse. One Easter season, staff and patients in the hospital where I was working were enjoying decorating Easter eggs, and I happened to notice one particular woman who remained outside of the activity room. As I engaged her in conversation and asked if she would like to help us decorate the eggs, she refused to even enter the activity room. After talking a little more, she explained to me that she had recently recalled memories of childhood sexual abuse. With that information, I felt I could relate to her distress. Then she added that the advent of Easter had brought out another aspect of the abuse– it had happened around the time of Easter. I now had a clearer understanding of why she would not enter the room to help us decorate the eggs, even though part of her wanted to join us.

There are numerous triggers for memories of CSA: a honeymoon, delivery of a baby, a child who reaches the age of the mother when she was abused, persons who may remind the survivor of her perpetrator, certain locations, etc. Sexual abuse triggers seem to be common and troublesome. Surgeries can be extra complicated. Facing fear and dealing with trauma reactions are also triggers for many who suffer with childhood trauma histories.

Trigger #1: Sexual Intimacy

I believe that sexual matters, of all topics, are most personal. My mother often said there are three things a person should never talk about: politics, religion and sex. I talk plenty about religion, not a lot about politics, and about sex, only with my husband. When I returned from our honeymoon, a girl friend asked me to tell her all about it. I vowed then that I never would share such intimate sexual details with anyone but my partner. This matter is private–even sacred to me. I once attended a class on the sanctity of sexual relations taught by an instructor of religion. He related to us that he and his wife feel very close to God when they are physically close, whether as co-partners in the act of creation or when deeply expressing their love for each other. I believe the human body is an incredible miracle. I also believe our bodies are intended to function as fully as possible to contribute to our joy and well being.

As I have listened to women's heartaches as they share the negative effects of their CSA on present relationships, I have come to believe that sexual expression and physical intimacy can trigger flashbacks. I have encountered women who might be considered phobic about avoiding such triggers, especially when they have been expected, from a tender age, to please males. They may consider it their duty and have little regard for their right to enjoy intimacy.

Others have described problems with sexual intimacy because they feel disconnected from themselves, their body, feelings and emotions (called dissociation). This seems to allow them to remove themselves from the sexual experience. In addition, some women with CSA have described feeling betrayed by their bodies, and believe sex is dirty and to be avoided, or it represents their main source of love.

Changing these negative feelings and behaviors, I believe, is possible.

Trigger #2: Surgery, My Example of Regression

When considering possible triggers for past trauma, I realized by my own powerful example that surgery can be an extra traumatic event. It makes sense, yet I did not understand the correlation until I faced a major operation. I had a very difficult time trusting the surgeon. I had never really trusted any man, and this one had control over my ability to walk correctly again and, for that matter, over my life. I remember vividly my post-op visit to his office. I saw him laughing while talking on the phone to someone about his boat engine. Being weak and woozy kept me from carrying out my impulse to kick him in a private spot, so great was my anger toward him for what he had done to me, although he had, indeed, saved my life. Why did I take a victim stance? This doctor had shown tremendous interest in me. I had been a challenge to his surgical ability. Even so, I felt bedraggled, used and violated. Still, I could not identify the source of my anger.

Ten days past the surgery, something happened. The combination of a drug reaction to Cortisone, lack of sleep, fear that the operation had not relieved the brain stem pressure, and very low blood pressure caused me to break with reality. I returned to the place of believing if I talked I would die: I was three. I was in a state of total collapse. I was unable to communicate by talking and could not explain why to anyone.

My husband and my good friend, Pam, took me to a stress center within a community hospital in a nearby town. My fate rested in the hands of the bearded psychiatrist who met us in the admitting area, and in my husband's ability to be my mouthpiece. Fortunately, he did a good job of explaining my overwhelming circumstances. He even included the incest background. The pleasant doctor deduced that the Cortisone was the cause of the manic condition leading to exhaustion, and that it would wear off within the next four days.

Once I was settled in a bed, my companion and Pam left for home. I was at the mercy of the employees of the stress unit who, fortunately, were sensitive and caring.

An echocardiogram was performed as I lay there. I had forgotten about not speaking until the technician gave information about the results. "Oh yeah?" I exclaimed with interest. Then realizing I had talked without dying, I jumped up and, in my patient gown, threw my arms around the startled fellow. "I talked and didn't die!"

"That's right Ma'am," the startled technician answered.

There followed a weaning from the safety of my bed–first, as a frightened, helpless three-year-old, I would follow the nurses down the hall and back. The staff accepted my regression and offered quiet reassurance and protection. I did not know how to do some of the routine hospital functions. Another patient helped me fill out menus, locate items, and dial the phone. On day four I could read again. As the rapid thinking stopped, my mind began to clear. I was discharged on day ten with medication for anxiety and the reminder that it would take a while to desensitize.

Intensified Fear Reaction

For me, squarely facing fearful situations, including a fearsome past, was an important step in conquering fear. Avoiding things, people, places and memories that may trigger old fearful reactions can add fuel to phobic and anxiety reactions. Despite that, there are times in our lives that give us the challenge to face our most dreaded fears. The following incident triggered the effects of my childhood trauma. It also taught me about the mind's processing of fear.

Close Call

Mine was the only car heading south on the highway as I drove to the hospital to put in my eight-hour night shift. Classical music playing on my tape player contributed to my peaceful, unhurried state. Suddenly, sparks were flying and metal was crashing across the road in front of me as an oncoming, out of control car traveling northbound at 90 miles per hour plummeted over the median and across the road directly in front of me. Then all was silent as the vehicle lay upside down on the shoulder of the road. I stopped my car and turned my lights on the scene. I remember saying, "God, help me to help," as I exited my car feeling terribly alone. Three injured victims climbed from the shambles. They quickly noticed that one passenger was missing. I immediately ordered some teenagers, who had joined me after witnessing the accident, to search for the missing girl.

One of the young men called, "I found her . . . over here!"

I told the others to remain and I joined the trembling young man. The girl's body was a mass of tissue, ballooned by crushing injury and tossed almost out of reach into the blackberry bushes where the moonlight reflected her distorted form to our unbelieving eyes. As a nurse, I reached up to her foot for a pedal pulse. The foot was cold and mushy.

"Whadda ya think?" questioned the young man.

"I think she's dead, buddy." I replied.

We held onto each other, both shaking, as a woman from the next street yelled, "I've called an ambulance; don't move anyone!" Overpowered with the emotional situation and angry that not one other adult had stopped to assist me in this ordeal, I felt she was criticizing my efforts. I screamed to her at the top of my lungs, "I'm a nurse and I'm doing just fine!" And in truth, I continued to perform quite effectively, caring for the others until the ambulance arrived and helping distraught family members in the Emergency Room at the hospital. Not able to drive home, I even worked my night shift. However, the following morning a deep shock reaction began.

Our unit psychiatrist at the hospital explained that few of us come face-to-face with death as I had done the previous evening. He kindly prescribed a tranquilizer to ease my crying and vomiting. Still, for the following few days, my trauma seemed extreme. I was so afraid of the dark I could not look out the window at night or walk down an unlit hallway. I evidently was revisiting my past fears, as I felt like a helpless little child. I was afraid of being harmed and even of being responsible for the teenager's death somehow. My recovery involved cutting the girl's picture out of the obituary so I had a face to look at. I imagined talking with her. Even though I could not have saved her life, I apologized for not being able to try as her body had been caught high above me in the bushes. I attended her funeral and hugged her mother. By the following week, I was able to drive cautiously to work. I felt such gratitude that my life was spared and I appreciated the gift of life more fully.

Fear Can Be Useful

There is similarity between the fear I have described in dealing with the accident related above and my incest recovery. In both, I felt the terror repeatedly until I faced it, acknowledged it, and put it to rest.

At one point, I wanted to eliminate all fear from my life. I remember asking a hypnotherapist friend of mine to help me do away with all my fear. She explained that fear is a very useful emotion, protective and necessary for survival. Her words were reinforced for me one day when my car broke down. I was in a hurry to arrive on time for a class I was to teach at the hospital where I worked, so I greatly appreciated the assistance of the man who stopped and offered to help. Unable to start the car, he guided it to the roadside and offered to give me a lift. I jumped into his car without even thinking. Trusting in this case was a poor choice. As we drove, he began telling me in explicit terms how I could repay him for the favor, and I realized I was in trouble. I applied all my relaxation techniques to stay collected, ignored his words and prepared to exit quickly if he were to leave the main road leading to the hospital. I told him I had a hundred people waiting for my speech, when in reality only ten were awaiting my assignment. I collapsed with relief into the arms of the program director upon arriving safely at the hospital.

As significant as it is to face and deal with my fears, it is also important to learn how to let go of them. How easy it is to feel guilty about the morbid preoccupation with the terribles of our lives. "I just can't get this wonderful thought out of my mind" is a complaint I have never heard. I suspect I am not alone in the tendency to give tremendous power to unthinkable thoughts–the ones that scare me. My most exciting breakthrough has been the acknowledgment of the power and tenacity of my particular spirit. I am able to create my external environment to be comfortable, safe, and pleasant in appearance. Likewise, I can create my internal environment. I build upon my store of happy memories so I can draw upon it. Listening to the voice of fear and dread is not nearly as useful as hearing the voice of strength and hope.

CHAPTER 8

Depression

The Lady with the 'No Laughin' Eyes

Once upon a time, if you will excuse the fairy tale introduction, a young mother of five lived in a small farming community. Dutiful, caring, generous and responsible, Teresa was well-known for her fine, unselfish qualities. The children in the community saw her differently and would describe her as sad and lonely; in fact, they dubbed her as "the lady with the 'no laughin eyes'." Her eyes, indeed, were described perfectly. They never laughed, even when she laughed. Teresa became ill and restricted in her service to others. With the illness came a bout of depression for which she finally consented to seek treatment. She had never told a soul about her childhood and surprised herself by blurting out long buried resentment toward her cruel, perverted father. She was aware of his sexual abuse of her siblings and took strength in her belief, "but he never got to me!" In her own mind, the mistreatment in her home did not affect her. However, in her eyes, the windows of the soul, there was no laughter.

The reason that I refer to Teresa's story is that a common feature many people have described to me is the expression of pain in the eyes of the abused. "What's it about?" is the first question people ask when I reveal that I am writing a book. With the reply, "It's about abuse, primarily sexual abuse and incest," some immediately become silent as if the topic were taboo. However, most people, including many males, show an immediate interest and often add either a personal account or that of an acquaintance. Sad eyes are frequently included in the description of the abused person.

When I phoned my oldest son, Richard, with my then recently discovered history of abuse, I expressed such relief for gaining a better understanding of myself and told him nothing looked the same any more. He was so pleased that I felt validated and adventuresome, childlike and more loving. He responded to me warmly and expressed the hope that perhaps now the sadness in my eyes would be gone. And indeed, upon his next visit home, he told me he had never before seen such sparkle radiating from my eyes.

Antidepressants

I have known depression. Sometimes it sneaks up on me until I find myself confused, unsociable, unfocused and wanting to sleep long hours. I will go to bed without washing my face or brushing my teeth, ignoring the rituals of self-care and effective living. My antidepressants of choice are:

- **Exercise**
  One of the many benefits of exercise is that it raises the seratonin level in the blood and elevates the mood. For me a brisk 30-minute walk, either alone or with a friend, will often lift my mood noticeably. When anxiety accompanies my depression, I get onto my exercise bike or the rebounder (mini-trampoline) and workout for 20 minutes for the natural antianxiety benefit that lasts for several hours.

- **Expression**
  Being able to have a long talk with my husband, a trusted friend, a relative (often a sister) or a therapist, has been helpful when I feel I am slipping into old patterns of depression. Whenever I am moving to a new area, I establish a support system as quickly as possible. Having friends close by to share with also keeps our long distance phone bill more manageable! Prayer is another form of expression which eases my troubled mind and lifts my level of depression. In addition, writing continues to be a powerful method of getting myself back to where I want to be.

- **Food**
  Sugar, for me, is a depressant that can rapidly swing my mood into despair, so I try to avoid foods that contain a lot

of sugar–my personal simple carbohydrate toxin. Eating complex carbohydrates has a calming effect. Raw vegetables remain my favorite munchies. I used to provide them for my teenage sons' parties to counter the junk food abundantly supplied. I have continued through the years to be known as "The Veggie Mom". (My suspicious sons insist the healthy whole wheat and molasses cookies I make also have sprouts and broccoli in them.) I admit that ordering a pizza after attempting to eat some of my health-producing meals has been a welcomed break. Nevertheless, I continue to study nutrition and to increase our health and well being through foods.

- **Rest**
A nap with the phone unplugged can do wonders as my anti-depressant. Sometimes my depression is due to plain exhaustion. A good night's sleep gives me a chance to awaken less depressed the next morning.

- **Medication**
When depression has me under its influence, I sometimes forget to do the things that would help me. The energy and desire to be uplifted are diminished. With long standing depression, as during my illness, I was grateful for a prescribed anti-depressant, which I used faithfully for two years and then tapered off gradually. Anti-depressant drugs have improved in treating depression symptoms. They helped to remind me of how it felt to be alive again and of having the light on inside of me. The combination of an anti-depressant and therapy made my recovery move more quickly than either did alone.

I most definitely dislike depression–my joy killer and my distracter. Nevertheless, it has taught me some interesting strategies.

Time out

When you quit having dreams, or hopes, or plans, that's depression.

Juanita, recovering survivor

Following the birth of my fifth son, a bout of depression drove me to therapy. As a nursing mother attempting to garden, preserve foods, make butter, bake bread and tend to the other four children and household tasks, I was over extended and drained. I blurted to the counselor, "It feels like everyone is nursing from me." My milk was about to dry up. I could relate to only one area when we attended the local county fair that year: I spent an hour leaning against a stall containing a mama pig with all her babies getting their nourishment from her. I learned a lot that day as I identified with that pig. I needed to make some changes.

My therapist suggested a plan I initially felt would be impossible to implement. I was told to do absolutely nothing short of caring for my baby. My husband was instructed to recruit the other children and carry on the household and farm tasks without Mom. He explained to them, "Mom needs a break." I needed a break in order to avoid a breakdown. My therapist assured me it would work. Even when I was working at the local hospital, they gave us a number of mental health days off.

My therapist's instructions were: "You don't have to get dressed. You do not have to make the bed. You do not have to apply makeup. You do not have to cook or clean. Don't do anything you do not want to do."

"But," I wailed, "what if I never want to?"

"You will", she replied, "when you are ready."

Initially, I stayed in my robe all day as if I were physically sick. I closed all the curtains and removed the phone from the hook. The family survived quite nicely with their mom on strike. On day three I felt the urge to cook dinner. On day four I did cook dinner. It was such a relief to be *choosing* to cook. I weaned myself from the couch back into a life with choices. One of my choices was to keep each Thursday as my own mental health day. At first, I spent my mental health day in seclusion, reading and listening to music. I then included window-shopping and lunch with a friend. My so-called "do nothing" days were probably the days during which I accomplished the most.

IV

RECOVERY

Incest sends us on a journey of leaving ourselves and recovery is our return.

Thia, survivor, psychologist

CHAPTER 9

Physical Recovery

The Power of Touch

Don't Touch Me, It Hurts

While driving through town one day, I pulled up behind a mangled little Volkswagen that obviously had been involved in an accident. On what remained of the bumper, a sticker read, "Don't touch me, it hurts".

For those of us with a CSA background, touch can be a difficult area with extremes ranging from avoiding it, to having insatiable needs.

The message on the bumper sticker was clear, the damage was visible and it worked. I kept my distance! Then I thought about how I had been abused just like the Volkswagen, and both of us had signs of that abuse. The difference in the signs is that they were obvious with the VW; with me, they were not so obvious, at least not visible. My own experience demonstrated how well abuse could be concealed. To others, I conveyed an image of competence and of having it all together. I guess you might call it a polished exterior. In fact, my exterior, or how I presented myself, was so polished that even I believed it. What I have been able to piece together since I began the journey to recovery is that somewhere deep inside of me I was never truly happy. Something had been missing but I did not know what. It was so distressing for me to learn that those to whom I should have been close were confused by my avoidance of closeness, and at times of not wanting to have others touch me, literally or emotionally.

One particular day at our house my family observed that the dog seemed to be getting the most attention. Every time she sauntered up to one of us she received pats and "Atta girl." We treat her well in our home, and she openly seeks attention when she needs it. Why is that so difficult for humans? In Steven Farmer's book, *Adult Children of Abusive Parents*, there is an excellent segment entitled, "HOLD ME: LEARNING TO TOUCH AGAIN" that includes journaling suggestions and ways to overcome touching problems.

For me, it is when I am out of touch that I experience greater pain. By this I mean that, on occasion, I do run out of the ability to touch and be touched. How sad to not receive and give appropriate touch. It causes us as much harm as not getting enough sleep or not eating properly. Human pats and hugs need to be increased. The bumper sticker that reads, "Have you hugged your kid today?" certainly beats the one on the Volkswagen, "Don't touch me, it hurts".

Hug Power

I met Gina while I was attending training in a university setting a number of years ago. Approximately 30 women and two men were taking a course to prepare us for conducting support groups of incest survivors in communities throughout the United States. Our instructor divided us into smaller groups and had us practice effective methods in facilitating groups. At each session, we would choose a new topic for discussion. One happened to be the issue of touch. At the end of the session, we decided to give and receive hugs from each other. Gina let us know none of us were to touch her, even with a friendly hug. Her history was especially devastating and although she longed for affection, she felt the need to be guarded. Petite and mannerly, Gina did not wear a sticker as did the VW and she felt compelled to inform us about her injury, her fear of being close to another human being. As the sessions continued, the level of trust increased, and the time came to move on to another group. I cautiously approached Gina and asked, "What would happen if I gave you a hug right now?" Tears filled her soft blue eyes. Not only did she agree to accept my hug, but she also received a hug from each of the other group members.

After a couple of other similar experiences, I wrote the following words:

Let down, dear sister
 years of tears.
Cries ignored

will now be heard.
Let go the grief
    'tis not in vain.
Tears with understanding
    bring relief.

Hold tight, dear one
    grown, yet small.
This, too, will pass
    Tho' night seems long.

Let down, dear sister,
    years of tears.
Tears with understanding
    bring relief.

Hugs are my favorite manifestation that we share our trials and strengths–that I am not alone. If I could hold in my arms a dear sister in need right at this moment, and if we could share a compassionate hug, strength would come. When there is no one there to hold me, those are the times I will hold on to myself with a long, tight hug. There are also times when I envision myself being held in the arms of God. By combining human feelings in this way, divine emotions speak inexpressible words to our spirit.

Massage Therapy

Following a car accident, my insurance company told me to get all the massage treatment I could for the next few weeks to reduce the trauma. My massage therapist was happy to accommodate and taught me a great deal about deep muscle tissue injury. As a result, I did not suffer with whiplash, had little pain, and recovered quickly. We often discussed the merits of massage, the most surprising to me being the natural release of tension and anxiety from the cells.

For me, massage was a quality-of-life saver. Following my surgery, I developed chronic pain syndrome, which had reached the point of semi-disability when I started treatment. The doctor asked my husband to give me massages three times each week. He explained that the naturally occurring release of endorphins resulting from massage would decrease my pain and depression. My husband and I enrolled together in a class on massage at the local YWCA, where we learned about various techniques and oils to use. "Heavenly" is the closest term I can use to describe my regular massages. In addition, the price was right! Massage encourages the body to call upon all of the tremendous restoration and healing processes that lie within every one of us.

CHAPTER 10

Emotional Recovery

We All Have Scars

Several years ago, a precious, good-looking, young nephew of mine received injuries in an automobile accident. He sustained multiple lacerations of the face and required over 90 stitches in an effort to repair the damage. I sent him a get-well card, and his sincere response has impressed me to this day.

"Dear Aunt Victoria, thank you for your card. I am doing fine. I just wonder if and when the scars will go away."

In response to his short and poignant letter, I wrote: "Jeremy, we all have scars resulting from mishaps, accidents, and tragedies of various types. Some are very deep, but not visible. You are not alone in wondering if and when your scars will heal. As a nurse, I have seen even elevated and discolored scars fade, with time, into a pale line. The scars remained, but rather than representing tragedy, they became a symbol of healing."

I suspect many have asked when their scars will heal. My experience leads me to believe that some people may never completely recover from the injuries of his or her past. Emotional and physical scars may remain, but they can represent healing rather than tragedy. I made the mistake of picking at my wounds for several years, unnecessarily digging at my abuse and feeling sorry for myself. I believed somehow I was permanently damaged. I thought if I worked harder, I would heal faster. It took me a long time to realize the continual picking only served to make the wounds deeper and prevent them from healing.

It is interesting to note that healing from abuse seems to follow the pattern of grief work:

- Denial
- Anger
- Bargaining
- Depression
- Acceptance

Why on earth, would there be a need to grieve the loss of memories of child abuse? They have been extremely painful. We suffer losses every day of our lives, and the grief process is necessary for us to move forward. Looking at the loss in a different light helped me to put it into perspective: I was grieving the loss of my childhood, not the loss of the memories. The memories will always be a part of me, but I have to create my childhood anew. Why would it be necessary to create my childhood anew? Because I learned to deal with my reality by developing a variety of defense mechanisms that got me by as a child, but which have been dysfunctional as an adult. Recovery required that I eliminate those behaviors that no longer serve a purpose for me and develop better ways of dealing with life's experiences. As an adult, I can make more informed decisions about my experiences than I did as a child.

Another phase in my recovery process involved my holding onto the belief that I was special–indeed, almost superior for having survived my childhood drama. With or without a background of CSA, each individual is unique. I resist the notion that my identity is as a woman who has been sexually abused.

The manner in which I treat my wounds determines my personal path toward healing. My recovery is realized when I walk with my family of brothers and sisters on this earth, feeling no better and no worse than those around me.

Self-Discovery-Coming Back to Myself

Picture This

Upon entering my home, you will see sitting on my "family memory table" an oval-framed picture of two-year-old Victoria. Dressed in a striped pinafore, with her hair in short wispy curls, an impish grin captures her delight.

One of my main goals in therapy was to be able to recapture the joyfulness of the child within this frame. Her innocence tells me that more important than establishing a perpetrator's guilt is to believe and firmly plant my innocence in my mind. I have studied Little Victoria and have imagined what she was like before the nightmares began.

My picture represents my God-given right to be me, to be free, to feel and to express. My childhood picture reminds me that skinned knees do heal, cotton candy messes are worth it, watching sow bugs curl into balls is a miracle, and the tooth fairy will come. Looking at Little Victoria is a way of coming back to myself–of recapturing the original me.

Viewing pictures of my parents as children also helped. Mother's impoverished childhood only has a few recorded pictures, and she is not smiling. She does not like my favorite picture of her, which I had enlarged and framed. Yet, when she looks at the picture, she does remember how warm her first winter coat felt. My heart goes out to the young child in her first warm coat at the age of four. My father was a beautiful baby with perfect features. Even my grandfather was once an innocent, handsome child with pudgy little legs. Who am I to know what situations caused him to make poor choices? Over the years, bitterness within me has lessened as I view these pictures.

Overcoming Fear

Over the Edge

Watching the young men, women, and an occasional parent descending from the 150-foot cliff, inch around the outer ledge, and then rappel to the earth below was of great interest to me. My own children followed one another into the depths below. I refused to look down, not wanting to view how far the descent actually was.

"Ok, Victoria, it's your turn," called my son's friend, Mitch.

Wow! Did I have the courage to go over the edge? Other observers warned me I should try a smaller cliff for my first attempt at rappelling. Actually, I felt it did not matter how far the distance between the top and bottom of the cliff. The tricky part was overcoming the fear of "going over the edge" and then making my way along the underside of the cliff in order to begin the actual descent. Being an instructor in the skills of overcoming anxiety and fear, how could I avoid conquering this one? What an opportunity to apply the principles–access my strengths from within myself. See myself successfully rappelling. Feel the thrill. "I'll do it!" I declared.

Mitch secured the belt around my waist, "See this clamp? It will hold your weight. Nothing will cause it to break". He gave me a five-minute lesson, concluding with the reminder that he would be going down with me on a separate rope at the same time–and there I stood on the edge.

"Now, just lean back and let yourself go. TRUST," Mitch advised.

I had to trust. Trusting was not one of my natural inclinations. I had to trust Mitch, the rope, the hitch, the person below, and my legs to keep me from crashing into the rocky cliff. Trusting myself to remember the instructions and knowing I had a great deal of responsibility for my safety was a heavy burden. I leaned back and crept over the edge. "Are you okay, Victoria?" Mitch called after my initial descent.

"I'm just praying," I replied.

He yelled to the others waiting and watching above us, "She's fine, just praying."

"Are you sure I can do this, Mitch?" I questioned.

"Yep." He answered reassuringly.

"Okay, with you as my guide, I'm ready." I continued and felt the thrill of conquering fear. With the sky as my backdrop, the breeze beckoned me. Like a bird on its first flight, I moved timidly at first, and then I soared. The feat was symbolic of my undaunted spirit.

I wanted the pleasant ride to continue, but my far-reaching vision was soon limited by surrounding cliffs. "You're almost to the bottom," came a familiar voice from below. My son, Ryan, who controlled the rope at the end, called out to his friends, "Be careful. She's a grandma and she's my mom!"

My feet touched the earth. I heard cheers from above and around me. My husband and children were pleasantly surprised and proud of me. As a once worrisome child who had developed into a fearful adult who avoided adventure, this was a big step for me.

Making Peace with the Night

> *Sleep my child and peace attend thee;*
> *All through the night.*
>
> Old Welsh Lullaby

Sleeping can be a problem for those of us who have been abused. I know my childhood gave me every reason to feel frightened at night. I had frequent, repetitive dreams about fire. Often I awoke unable to see my hands. I thought they were black from burns, and I would have to check them out by turning on a light. I felt I was a very bad person, and this was attached in some way. The first prayer I was taught to recite each night didn't help matters either:

Now I lay me down to sleep
I pray the Lord my soul to keep
If I should die before I wake
I pray the Lord my soul to take.

I remember climbing into bed after my prayer and wondering "Will tonight be the night I will die?"

It seems to be common for individuals with an abuse history to have nightmares about monsters. Of course, other little children do also. Perhaps that is why we may not attach much significance to them unless the nightmarish themes follow us into adulthood. I learned a great deal from an article I read years ago about the monsters in children's dreams. One night when my son had a nightmare, I had the opportunity to test the advice I had read. I turned on the light and told him to draw the monster, and then he would not have that dream again. He drew a hideous purple monster with green fangs and described how awful it was, and then he went back to sleep. The next morning he said the monster did not return. To my knowledge, I am not aware that it ever has.

For me, the following poem has been useful in facing some of my monsters:

It's my own I'm not able to forgive I'd like to make peace with
all the dragons in my head –
all those dark creatures
who came in the open door of childhood
and bedded down.
I've denied them, feared them, and fought them,
All the same, I've fed them rather well.
They've grown fat on my hatred,
Multiplied like rabbits in the warm nest of my obsession,

Overpopulated my psyche with their kids.
I'm very kind to other people's dragons,
I'm holding all my dragons by their tails-
I'd like to meet them face to face,
get to know them,
where they came from,
why they came.
It's hard to love my enemies, Lord-
To make peace with intrusive creatures
who moved in first
then signed those long-term leases in my head.
Please come in and help me face the dragons,
(help me not to run if they breathe a little fire),
I'd like to meet a really scaly monster
shake his hand
maybe even smile.
You know I'm not some princess in a palace,
Who thinks it's rather nice to kiss a frog.
But if I learn to love that ugly dragon,
Could you change him to a prince before too long?

Anonymous

I found it helpful to think back to some of the dreams and fears I had when I was a child and to make peace with the darkness. I was dealing with a terrified little child who needed consistency and consoling, positive self-talk and reassuring. It was necessary to provide myself with whatever I needed to get in touch with feelings of security. Holding onto something such as a pillow or a stuffed animal or leaving a crack in the door so the light could come in helped the child in me face the unknown.

I have learned to let sleep be a very refreshing time. If I awaken during the night, I try to use that time to ponder if there is something I need to deal with on a deeper level of my consciousness. Often, I turn to prayer during these moments. I suppose many of my increasingly delirious prayers do not really get to the desired destination, but it is still helpful for me to silently pray as I drift into sleep. Another method for overcoming sleeplessness is to say, "I love you" as you breathe in and again as you breathe out very slowly. I had been practicing this relaxing method long before I read about it. This has a very calming effect.

Rather than panicking and thinking, "Oh no, I'm not going to get enough rest, and tomorrow I'll be cross, tired and I won't be able to function," I can tell myself, "Here is an opportunity. I wonder what nice thing is in store for me this early hour when the house is quiet and the children are asleep?" Then, I just let it happen. Sometimes, during that trance-like state, wonderful and pure ideas come to me.

There are numerous additional helps for falling asleep, such as reading a boring book, playing a relaxation tape, drinking warm milk, counting ten long, relaxed breaths–each one leading into deeper relaxation. I also recognize it is sometimes necessary to use sleep medication. Tranquilizers and sleeping pills, used appropriately, can be helpful. My concern, however, is that I not let it become a habit.

Recapturing Delight

Tis a gift to be simple
Tis a gift to be free
Tis a gift to come down
Where we ought to be
And when we find ourselves
In the place that's right
Twill be in the valley
Of love and delight
                    Nineteenth Century Shaker Hymn

In looking back into my life, it was as if I was merely imitating others' reactions. I had a continual gnawing sense of being a fake, of covering over my real self. I felt like a great pretender, an actress, alone among real people with whom I did not truly belong. Dr. Ron Minson explained that my dysfunctional childhood held onto the pain and kept the joy and good out. Therefore, my childhood was not real in a sense. As my insulation from childhood pain thinned, my joyful times increased without pretense.

When my therapist told me I would be a lot happier now that the once-buried secret of my abuse was out, I had no idea how much fun was ahead. Fortunately, I had a window of time between rediscovering my abuse and the onset of brain stem pressure symptoms. I filled my six-month reprieve with physical activity, long walks, race walking classes, dancing, and bike rides.

I went on a bike ride one afternoon and rode for hours through miles of gorgeous countryside, drinking in the splendor with full awareness of my surroundings. Only leg muscle exhaustion caused me to pull over into a little gas station to call my husband to come and get me. When he asked, "Where are you?" I honestly did not know. I had to ask the attendant. What I did know was I felt delight for the first time. I felt like a little girl again, in a healthier way.

Following the surgery to relieve the brain stem pressure, I was unable to ride a bike. Then I discovered the thrill of going down slides and swinging on swings. My boys were aware of this, and as we drove along in our family station wagon, they would shout, "Mom, swings and a slide!" whenever they spotted a playground. We would pull over and play. I could not hold back my gleeful delight, especially when going down the curly slides.

Goin' for the Go-cart

I suppose my son figured I was ready for the next step when he introduced me to the world of go-carts. "Hey, Mom, wanna have some real fun?" implored my ten-year-old son, Ryan. "Come and ride on a go cart with me. You'll love it." His invitation opened the door into personal bliss. I had never experienced a more thrilling activity than to sit behind the wheel of our incredible go-cart. I felt like one of the kids, and I was 44 years old. Later, I realized by participating in these activities, I was indeed taking care of Little Victoria by recreating my childhood into a happier one.

After our go-cart ride, I announced to Ryan, "I want one!"

His eyes lit up, "Me too, Mom. Let's buy one. I've saved 20 dollars. I'll go in with you. We'll drive around and around our farm until there will be a path to use. It'll be great!"

With our front footage already converted into a soccer field for Trent and his soccer buddies, my husband agreed to sacrifice a bit of the hayfield. Now we were lacking only the vehicle. I called my father and told him of my recent major flashback, that I had never had fun as a child, and that I was finally able to experience the real thing. I ended with my go-cart experience and right out asked if he would buy us one. He agreed to pay for most of our go-cart.

Upon moving from the farm into a residential neighborhood, we had to surrender our go-cart, so my husband built a huge swing for me. One of my greatest pleasures during my rehabilitating years was swinging on that homemade swing.

I love the opportunities I receive to return to childlike delight!

I Am a Treasure

At the end of each of my sister's aerobic classes, she invites participants to give themselves a hug and say aloud, "I am a treasure!" I have followed her example by including this practice in my classes and home visits. I love to witness the resulting change in their countenances as people hug themselves and repeat the message affirming their great worth. The warmth and smiles produced by such a simple act inspired me to write the following story depicted from my farmhouse view of rainbows. It is, I think, a fitting conclusion for this chapter on emotional healing.

Golden Treasure

The heavy-laden clouds had already released their soft blankets of rain when she gazed upon the earth's renewal from the neatly framed farm window. A brilliant display of color arched itself across the newly cut hay field. The rainbow caused the young woman to return to her childlike fantasy in which she ran until too weary to reach the end of the rainbow and claim the treasure available to her as the true seeker.

She noted exactly where the rainbow's end touched down upon the landscape between the forest edge and the lone tree stump. Though she knew the notion was silly, she reached for her jacket and made her exit, tingling with excitement and curiosity. She had been teased about treasures, leprechauns, and even Santa, yet she was mysteriously drawn across the damp grass toward the forest edge by the stump.

A lengthy pause and then she fell to her knees in gleeful delight. A flat rock served her well as she scooped the soft mud to the side. While digging, she dared to hope beyond the boundaries of practicality. Deeper she dug, even deeper into the brown clay. A "clank" startled her, revealing a black lid, rusty and worn, on a metal pot. Gingerly, she removed the lid and tossed it with high hopes of having finally found the true reward, perhaps gold. Instead, near emptiness met her searching hand. She held the only content of the pot, a weathered strip of parchment with a scarcely readable message upon it: *I am a treasure to behold.* "I am a treasure to behold? And this is all?" she wailed. "What of my effort, hopes and dreams?"

Disappointed, she clasped the tattered paper to her heart, crying, "I came so close to finding a treasure." Yet, something happened as her free flowing tears fell upon the printed words causing a change to occur. Her body filled with the sweetest confidence, golden warmth, and richness unlike any had ever known. The moments passed uncounted. Still kneeling in the field, she discovered that the message was no longer visible. The blank paper was returned to its proper place in the blackened pot, with the lid secured and covered with moist earth.

The return to her farmhouse was a profoundly rich experience, so heavy was her treasure of gold. With each step, she vowed to be generous in sharing it with all.

Dear sisters, be willing to chase your dreams, to dig a little deeper, and discover for yourself that you are, indeed, a treasure to behold.

CHAPTER 11

Spiritual Recovery

Revenge

Whenever I watch talk shows about incest, I become a bit uncomfortable with the sensationalism accompanying such reviews. Yes, I believe it is important to increase public awareness of a national epidemic and that it is all right to talk about what happened; but recounting explicit detail in order to get even with the perpetrator does not make sense as a means of recovery and finding personal peace. There are many different views on these issues and, certainly, anyone has the freedom to scream and shout whether in a secluded room or on national television.

Fantasizing about a five-year imprisonment for the person who offended me or even a $100,000,000 check could not erase what happened. Even the perpetrator's death did not compensate me or make things suddenly better. Feelings that the offender should be required to pay for my therapy or, at the very least, ordered to write a full confession of the crime, did not help. But to what degree could I ever get even? Bitterness, hatred, and mistrust were common emotions and if I did not deal effectively with them, they only increased my injury and victimization. I, too, experienced anger, but over time I have accepted the reality that the only way to get even is to get well. The bottom line is that my offender was likely sexually violated also. It was important for me to realize he hadn't the tools to break the abuse cycle.

After my first major flashback, I came across a book written by Dr. Carlfred Broderick, *My Parents Married on a Dare and Other Favorite Essays on Life*. Someone had asked him this question: *So many children are abused, offended and abandoned. If little children are precious to God, what justification can there be for permitting some to be born into such circumstances?"*

His response was:

"As children of God, we have been given the great gift of choice. We may choose to help, or we may choose to hurt. Unfortunately, as the Lord explained to Moses, the iniquities of one generation are often visited upon the heads of following generations (Exodus 20:5). Anyone can see the truth of that saying by looking at many families in the world today. Often, troubled families seem to pass on their pain and darkness virtually intact to their children and grandchildren. The victim of one generation becomes the victimizer of the next.

On the other hand, the Lord told the prophet Ezekiel 18: 2-4: 'What mean ye, that ye use this proverb concerning the land of Israel, saying, The fathers have eaten sour grapes, and the children's teeth are set on edge? As I live, saith the Lord God, ye shall not have occasion any more to use this proverb in Israel.

Behold, all souls are mine; as the soul of the father, so also the soul of the son is mine: the soul that sinneth, it shall die. ' This scripture suggests that children need not merely replicate the sins of their fathers, but that each generation is held accountable for its own choices.

In Romans 12:19 we read, "Dearly beloved, avenge not yourselves, but rather give place unto wrath: for it is written, Vengeance is mine; I will repay, saith the Lord.[1]

It took me a while, but I choose now to allow my perpetrator to face the Savior and let Him mete out the punishment.

Forgiveness

Initially, forgiveness was an overwhelming word, implying a total cleansing of all negative feelings toward my offender. Being a religious person, I often believed if I did not forgive the perpetrator, I was the sinner. Then there was the guilt, "How awful I must be to want to be angry and to punish him."

For a long time, forgiveness was not in my vocabulary. In my readings, I came across many sources which described it as a long process and very difficult for most victims of sexual abuse. That point of view confirmed my personal experience. I wish that my system had let go of my pain in this area sooner. My life would have been easier. I did not have present-day resources available that teach effective release of negative emotions as found in Karol Truman's book, *Feelings Buried Alive Never Die.*

Hearing a powerful talk about forgiveness once caused me to cry for hours. I asked my husband, "Do you think I'll have to forgive my grandfather?" "Yes, dear" he replied. So, even though Grandpa was dead, I composed a letter, which my husband carefully read at my request.

"Victoria, this letter says 'I forgive you,' but it sounds like 'I forgive you, you blankity blank.' It says the word 'forgive,' but the anger is obvious. We laughed, because it really was awful. Writing the letter had been therapeutic. It showed me I was not yet in a place of forgiveness. In the Family section of this book is my second letter, written many years later to Grandpa, that indicates positive signs of forgiveness. The "softening" eventually brought about amazing peace, incomprehensible during the first phases of discovery.

If your desire to forgive is sincere, trust that it will be recognized and met in perhaps unusual ways that will eventually bring peace. For me, it followed an acceptance of what happened to me as a child and of my feelings and reactions. Forgiveness has been my process of accepting and then letting go of the pain that was associated with the perpetrator. It has involved recognizing his unhealed pain. More importantly, it has also involved self-forgiveness, allowing it to be my gift to myself.

Notes

1.Dr. Carlfred Broderick, Essays *My Parents Married on a Dare and Other Favorite Essays. (Holy Bible,* King James version, used throughout quotation).

CHAPTER 12

Therapy

Group Therapy

Therapy groups can be very effective for CSA survivors, as they give a sense of belonging, feeling safe, and not being alone with their issues. As is true of any type of clinical therapy, the most benefit is derived if the therapist is well trained in leading groups of individuals who have been sexually abused. Someone who is not well trained can cause even more trauma. Beware of those groups that perpetuate the negative aspects of abuse and where anger extends week after week after week. These tend to encourage the negatives and interfere with the healing process.

Group Non-Therapy

A great idea came to me one afternoon as I was listening to some humorous "how to be more positive" audiotapes: Why not share these with a group of friends? This, of course, could not be a therapeutic group, simply a support group. It would have nothing to do with abuse of any kind. The problem was, I did not know many women in the neighborhood that well. Yet, this would give me an opportunity to get to know them better. I got on the phone and called acquaintances. The woman who had recently moved into a house on the corner seemed sad and lonely. When I called, she accepted the invitation to attend our first meeting. I called a woman who was suffering with a recently diagnosed rare illness–another "yes". I then called the wife of a physician whose reserved manner intrigued me. She agreed to come. Number four was a gregarious, sometimes brutally honest friend in a neighboring town. The woman who lived four houses from me, my walking buddy, also consented.

The six of us had our first meeting at my house. The tape listening flopped, but the visiting and idea sharing flourished. We tried potluck lunches–too much work. Better to go out to lunch once a month and to celebrate birthdays. Together we shared goals and ideas, and reported on our successes of the previous week. We laughed a lot, and we were there for each other during crises. Our meetings continued for several months. The best get-together was when one member sang a farewell song she had written for us about friends. There was not a dry eye. I gained a great deal from the informal, non-professional meetings. Our two focal points were consistent sharing and being good listeners to one another.

The Tomatis Method

Have you ever had a fascination for a certain country or area you have never visited? I had been known to fantasize about running away to Denver, Colorado. People would ask, "Do you have family there?"

"No."

"Friends?"

"No, I've never even been there."

"Then why do you want to go there?"

"I haven't a clue, but some day I'll go."

In the fall of 1992, a kind hearted, innovative psychiatrist in Denver received my phone call. "Dr. Minson", I began, " because you have helped my sister overcome her depression, and I, also, seem to be plagued with depression, I'm wondering if your program might be helpful to me." He listened to my condensed personal history, ending with my unresolved illness. I shared with him my frustration that my therapist and doctors seemed to believe I had come a long way, but the pain and anxiety that followed my brain surgery would likely continue indefinitely.

In his reply, Dr Minson offered: "I disagree. I believe there is more that can be done to help you recover more fully, Victoria." He explained his continual amazement at how the Tomatis program supports and fosters individual insight, catharsis, and healing, with minimal involvement of a therapist. However, when invited, he would be available to further support the process. He also explained, "This is much more satisfying than the tedious methods of my traditional training. This approach to personal growth allows people to experience their potential and become who they really are." When he said that he had witnessed tremendous strides in freeing women from sexual abuse issues through the art and listening therapy used at the Tomatis Center, I determined I would find a way to get to Denver.

Finding my way

Each of us has our own path to recovery. In sharing the Tomatis experience, I do not mean to imply this method is for everyone. Because our desires, needs, readiness and willingness to grow vary tremendously, it is important we follow our own directives in selecting healing methods. I am truly grateful to be living in an era of expanding awareness, compassion and respectful treatment methods for someone who has experienced what I have. Dr. Minson permitted me to interview several women who, like me, had some unresolved abuse issues. Because I was fortunate in being able to experience this type of therapy, I am sharing the following experience as a sample of another method of health assistance.

Upon entering the Center for InnerChange (formerly known as the Tomatis Center), I felt the exhilaration, coupled with the dread of the unknown. Following a warm greeting, an evaluation with Dr. Minson to review my symptoms, concerns and goals, and a brief listening test, I was provided with specialized earphones that delivered specific Mozart selections; whereby the frequencies of the music were filtered and modified based on the results of my listening test. While listening, I proceeded to experiment with the provided painting supplies, drawing whatever came to mind. I wondered how this process, performed for two hours each day for two weeks, would relieve my suffering. The kind couple I was staying with was dubious as well initially, yet they provided me with food, lodging and taxi service to the center and supported my desire to recover and one day write this book. A critic friend of theirs remarked pointedly to me, "You're supposed to pray about problems to get help." I replied, "I did, and for me this was the answer, or I certainly would not be here."

Listening daily to the pure, yet specifically filtered, refrains of the

master composer, made me appreciate Mozart's contribution to my
well-being, and to this day, his music enlivens my spirit. It is no
wonder music is referred to as the 'language of the soul'. Sarah Jane
Stokes, in the book, *Music and Miracles,* by Don Campbell,
beautifully describes how the great music of the masters has
miraculous healing power that allows one to become more whole and
alive.

My Progression

A different kind of awareness occurred as I participated daily in
the Tomatis Program that included, filtered music, air and bone
conduction, consultations and changes based on my clinical progress
and listening tests. I felt as though miracles were happening. The staff
commented on how they had noticed I was sitting and standing taller
and that my posture had noticeably improved. Unspoken emotions
gushed forward from deep within me. When I was painting, it seemed
as though the faces, figures, and fanciful designs flowed from my
paintbrush. My original drawings contained primarily red color in
gruesome, haunting designs. Eventually, the colors softened, and then
they became bright and clear.

In the wee hours of the morning on day four of listening to
Mozart, my clenched fists, which seemed to tighten each night in my
sleep, opened and became soft and relaxed. I stared at my hands for
an hour, amazed with the relief, while wondering why and how this
had occurred. Apparently, something within me was getting resolved,
relaxed or feeling safe.

On day five, I received positive evidence that additional changes
were taking place. For years I had recognized a mild form of
dyslexia, in that my sense of direction was impaired; and I could
never recall quickly which hand was left and which was right. During
my listening time on the fifth day, it became clear to me there was no
longer any delay in knowing my right hand! With great excitement, I
painted hands and sunshine, long roads and rainbows. I greeted
Doctor Minson's wife and assistant, Kate, with gratitude and absolute
giddiness at my new ability. An improved sense of direction ensued. I
knew where I stood on the street, on a map, in the universe.

On day twelve, I felt I could see a new dimension. The simple
beauty of a snowfall enthralled me. I viewed every detail of my
environment with heightened awareness. Had I been given a drug

causing such a reaction, I would have desired a continual dose. I noticed that I felt increasingly connected to others through improved communication. My ability to really listen and pay attention improved dramatically. I called my sons and apologized for being such a poor listener in the past. I went home with an appointment to return in one month. This would give me time to integrate and use my newly improved skills. My friends' comments were supportive: "Victoria, you are taller and more solid. It is like you are together and more whole. Even your voice has become richer."

Healing Continuum

One month after my initial program, I returned to Denver for additional treatment. On day three I experienced a flashback into an unspeakable hell. I suffered with helpless, lost feelings, during which I drew pale figures of little ballerinas with drooping heads and little reason to dance. My assigned staff member offered me comfort. After my designated two hours of listening and drawing, I left in a daze and walked to a nearby mall with intense, inexpressible sadness. Dressed in a long coat and warm knitted hat, with a forlorn look on my face and thoroughly exhausted, I fell asleep while sitting in a rest area of an enormous mall. A little girl poked me, "Are you dead, lady?" she questioned. There I sat, a professional nurse, a wife, a mother of six children, experiencing despair I had buried so long ago as a little girl.

"Shhh," her mother whispered, "I'll tell you later." I wondered what the mother would tell her daughter about me.

That night was one of confusing dreams, anxious awakenings, and prayers for the courage to continue the program. The phobic, almost paralyzing fear was also my motivation to continue. I reasoned, "Perhaps some day I'll be able to help others by continuing this process."

After listening to the details of my horrendous night, Dr. Minson offered words of encouragement and the reminder to trust the process without talking about it further. This was so foreign to the traditional therapy in which you talk and talk and talk about unresolved fears. I had to admit that talking about my fears would often increase, not lessen my anxiety.

My assigned listening room that day was in the children's play area. I prepared to face my monster–fear, once again. Surprisingly the terror did not return. That day my program included singing silly songs with a tape. Having no recollection of ever having been a silly, happy, carefree little girl, I relished moments of true delight. When reminded my time was completed, I made a request. "May I stay here and play during the lunch hour?" Permission was granted. Grabbing a brightly colored hat for my head, I proceeded to topple every toy container in sight and to put the toys into one big heap. Textures, colors, and feelings were heightened as I stirred my treasure with full sweeping arms until I was exhausted and filled with pleasure. Only the moment mattered. My past felt resolved. I could just be me.

I shall always appreciate Mozart, to whom I now like to refer as my *music mother*. I experienced a 'sonic birth' as his music delivered me into the richer world of increased sensory perception and joyfulness. I also value the ability to continue my auditory training with a home-based listening program, TLP (The Listening Program®).

Freedom to Create

Since childhood, my teachers have recognized my ability to readily draw or realistically paint anything I could see. Yet, when my high school honors art class instructors assigned the class to illustrate a passage from a book, my canvas remained bare while the other students created their paintings. I realized then that my art was limited to what my eyes could see and imitate. I could only copy what I saw.

One of the most exciting results of my healing journey has been the increased ability to be creative. After reading the book, *A Creative Companion*, How to Free Your Creative Spirit, by SARK, I wondered if I, too, had a creative style. At age 57, following some additional recovery work and my husband's encouragement to pursue my artistic activities, the part of me that had been dormant burst forward with colorful images and designs. The ability to illustrate with pen and watercolors became one of my greatest joys. With this gift, my brush creates a unique version of what my eyes see. Images for my second book, *"Hilda is Coming to My House Today"* have been drawn in childlike design, and surrounded with brightly colored patterns. When I presented my original pages to Toni, a buyer from my favorite bookstore in Denver, she challenged me to use the hand written draft as the final draft! Even with the imperfectly handwritten pages, it was acceptable. She claimed, "The *Dear Sister* book led you to the fun-loving *Hilda* book. The first is needed, the second book is wanted." She then sent me over to the creative section of the bookstore where I had a feast viewing delightful books also written in their creator's own imperfect penmanship. *Hilda* has now become my symbol of recovery–a happy sequel to my more serious book. My blank canvas days have been replaced with endless creations.

Anxiety Release

Those who have experienced the frightening and bewildering onset of an anxiety attack know it is rightly-named. With my first episode, I truly felt as if I were being attacked, or at least struck with an adrenaline shock as suddenly as if a bolt of lightning had hit me. If lightning had actually struck me, I would have known what hit me. Though I am a trained mental health nurse, it took the expertise of a compassionate psychologist to identify my reaction. He labeled it as free-floating anxiety, meaning it was difficult to explain at the moment it occurred. That was many years ago and the truth of my childhood abuse was yet to be unraveled.

Viewing Anxiety
Oh, that I had known then about the anxiety release technique demonstrated by Robert McDonald in 1994 in an NLP seminar I attended. He was teaching us that anxiety is a frightening picture we see in our minds. Initially, the picture may be at a distance, yet it becomes larger and closer to us as the anxiety level mounts.

I was no longer just an interested trainee observer. As he described anxiety, I could feel its entrance into my mind and, of course, the more I tried to push it away, the more it pursued and increased in effect. I confessed my distraction to Mr. McDonald during the break. Somehow, I recognized this was the perfect time to get much-needed resolution. I accepted his invitation to be a volunteer for the Anxiety Release Demonstration he was going to teach the group.

Don't Let Anyone Die
He had me tell the group what was troubling me. At that particular time, I was troubled with the fact that one of my children was ill, and I was expected to give him powerful medications regularly. I explained that before my first job as a graduate nurse, my mother had

warned me, "Don't let anyone die." Shortly after that admonition, a patient who had been comatose for three months died on my shift! Even though her death had nothing to do with my care, I went home ill. Administering drugs, even vitamins, to patients became difficult for me. I would check, recheck and re-recheck the amount, the patient, and the drug, always afraid of making an error that might result in death. Evidently, beyond my awareness, I made a connection between death and Mother's warning. With Mr. McDonald's assistance, I dared to look at it. Unbelievably, what I saw was the old nightmare of my mother with bared teeth and a knife in her hand coming toward me. Mr. McDonald immediately had me put the picture into postage stamp size and zoom it away from me. Then I explained to the group the history of this particular nightmare.

Capable and Cautious

Mr. McDonald expertly guided me through an experience of seeing myself as a competent nurse preparing hospital medications with self-assurance and accuracy. He then touched my shoulder to anchor the pleasant feelings. I sensed the warmth, caring, and respect that radiated from him and from an empathetic audience, and the work continued in a more playful fashion. Next, he had me condense the confident nurse image into a dot, place the dot within the bared teeth of my mother, and go "*Poof*" With his reassurance, I visualized my positive self overpower the fearful image. Using an NLP swish pattern, again and again, the visual scene was repeated until the sense of being capable, yet cautious, was firmly implanted. He then had me imagine preparing medications, administering pills and giving shots. I felt great! I had faced the intruding image and replaced it with the positive image of myself performing well.

The exhilaration of resolving that nightmare continued with me throughout the day. I was amazed, because I had been told it would haunt me for the rest of my life. I even tried to conjure up the old reaction until the thought came to me, "Leave it alone, Victoria, and enjoy the change." A skeptic in the class remarked she would believe in the process only if the results lasted for a year. I was content with the immediate relief.

The following day, Mr. McDonald questioned how I felt about giving medication. I was glad to report that imagining myself doing so brought me feelings of joyful competence. That confidence remains to this day as I administer medications. I have no doubt that anxiety is an approaching picture in the mind and, by looking at that picture and treating it effectively, anxiety is deleted at its source. The skillful use of his work increased my desire to help others afflicted with anxiety–so much so, I sought additional training in the use of these skills.

Self-Coaching

We Can All Be Hitters

As the mother of six boys, I have had a lot of experience with coaches. Some coaches have been excellent and have left a positive imprint on my sons' lives, as well as on my own. When my elementary age sons were first assigned to a team, the coach received a call from me. I tried to determine whether he or she was a nurturing coach, because if the person was critical and harsh, I really did not want my child to be on that team. That is how important I think a good coach is.

My favorite example of effective coaching occurred one summer as I attended one son's T-ball game. The enthusiastic female coach fed the team messages of much needed encouragement. I'll never forget her words as one little slump shouldered boy came to the bench after striking out: "Kenny", she declared, "You ARE a hitter." She then looked at her team sitting there on the bench and announced, "You are ALL hitters!" She beamed. "Every one of you can hit that ball." They believed her words and by the end of the season proved her right. They were all hitters.

You Can Be a Great Runner

My oldest son was the shortest runner on his high school cross-country team. His coach soon had him running as if he were as long legged as the other team members. He literally stood tall with the team (by standing upon a chair at their banquet) and to this day, he continues to love running. The coach assured him that with his determination, increased strength and endurance he could be a great runner. With that original message of his inspiring coach internalized, my son recently placed second in the Susitna 100-mile-race across frozen Alaska. I wonder what the result would have been if that coach had said, "You're too short to be a great runner?"

Breathe in Strength, Then Blow Out the Pain

I had an unexpected opportunity to coach a young man in desperate circumstances following a high school soccer accident. His severely broken leg brought on a state of deeply dangerous shock, and due to communication mix-ups, the paramedics were delayed in arriving at the high school. Two community doctors were with him on the field, yet his sister ran to the bleachers yelling, "They're losing my brother!" I ran to join them and, indeed, the boy was fading, pale and incoherent. I asked the doctors if I could work on his head while they dealt with his leg. I requested more blankets for increased body temperature and then put my mouth next to his ear and gave him clear instructions to listen to my voice and to breathe with me, nice deep breaths. I reminded him, "Your coach has taught you to be strong and capable. Breathe in that strength. Now, blow out the pain." Shortly, his color returned. As long as he paid full attention to the coaching, he was able to endure the suffering. Consistent, positive messages had worked for him. They work for all of us.

Being My Own Coach

We need to develop our ability to coach ourselves. Just as the critical voices of others eventually become our own, supportive voices can be reclaimed or created, and then increased in volume, intensity and duration. And, when we need them most, voila they are there!

Before the birth of my fourth son, I had worked part time as a labor and delivery nurse where it was my responsibility to assist women through the drama of bringing a child into the world. During the last stage of labor, the power of suggestion is heightened, and most women are dependent on clear, firm commands to get them through it. In learning what to tell my patients, I had ingrained within myself each step. When the time came for the delivery of my own son, I was my own coach saying, "Now it's time to pant, . . . blow out," and so on. I remember laughingly saying, "Look at me; I'm being my own delivery room nurse!" Under the extreme condition, the patterns were there. This was a powerful lesson in the ability to self-coach. What a blessing it has been to discover I do have a coach. I just had to train her to deliver more messages that are positive.

V

FAMILY

With many differing views, desires, and beliefs from my family members, one day I told my mother, "I feel like I was hatched in the wrong nest."

Over the years as I have accepted and loved so many of my family members, our "stands" have softened. In reflection, my original nest eventually encouraged my flight.

Victoria Lynn

CHAPTER 13

To Mothers

Can't You Just Think of a Rose?

Mother was totally shocked with the news of my abuse. I had traveled some distance to visit her in order to approach her face to face. But what I certainly could not communicate at age three, I could barely express at 42.

We walked together through the park near my mother and stepfather's home as I carefully related the major flashback experience and asked for her assistance–having so few memories of my childhood.

"You don't know for sure anything bad happened," Mother muttered. "You have such an imagination and the way you exaggerate . . . I don't know. If I thought about the things I know have happened to me in my life, I could be upset too, let alone worrying about what might have happened."

Heavily burdened, we walked along the tidy path leading through the garden toward the house. "Can't you just think of something pleasant, like a rose?" she questioned. Oddly enough, we were passing a rose bush as she spoke. I stared blankly at a coral-colored rose. I was appalled at her suggestion to simply switch my concern to the thought of a rose. A strange, haunting sensation overcame me. This was not the first time I had tried to tell Mother something was wrong. Even as a child, she had told me to think of something pleasant, (a rose, of all things) way back when. From my childhood memory came the same supplication, this time to a frightened child (myself) who could not sleep because of frightening nightmares. "Can't you just think of a rose?" Conversation ended. No wonder I disliked roses and ignored the aphids all those years.

There were books in which I read that the mother is always aware, at least on some level, of her child's abuse. I do not know if I agree. I have talked with moms who admit they knew, but many insist they did not know. I believe with the combination of co-dependency and denial, even the obvious becomes obscured. A mother's discovery of her daughter's abuse in some cases might trigger a tucked away memory of her own mistreatment or abuse. Being asked to look at her daughter's abuse when it unveils her own is a double whammy. I would imagine she might feel ill equipped to deal with it. My mother remembers an incident with her father when he came toward her in great anger carrying a stick, and that is all she remembers.

Although I had telltale symptoms, Mother admits she did not know what to look for, and certainly none of the doctors she took me to ever suggested I might have abuse trauma. She knew something was wrong with me and was willing to do anything to help me. She would not have sent me on Grandma's trips to join Grandpa had she known. In fact, Grandma was right in telling Grandpa, "If Wilma (my mother) finds out, she'll kill you." Mother was very protective; in fact, overprotective of me–her poor little girl who seemed to lack normal joy and affection.

It took a few months after my disclosure that day in the garden for Mother to request more information. I was pleased when she consented to join me in a therapy session. In the therapist's office, it seemed my own mother was a confused child hearing what seemed impossible for her to comprehend. I felt sorry for her, and it was embarrassing for both of us. The counselor was kind, yet explicit, in her defense of my position. She had to repeat the information several times. Mother was given some titles of books to read and later confessed they were "too deep" for her to understand. My mother is not ignorant or stupid. I just believe her mind had difficulty absorbing the information.

It takes courage to come from an era of "don't talk or even think about such things" to a position of "tell me again what happened to you." Every couple of years mother would bring up the abuse, and I would try to explain the unexplainable. Initially, I could hardly bear to talk about it; then I talked of little else during the various stages of working through it. In the process of writing this book, I have learned to close my abuse file, to put it into the drawer, and to concentrate more fully on gorgeous sunsets, babies' smiles, yummy dishes . . . so much beauty, laughter and joy to experience. Then when I am ready, I pull the file out and develop it a bit further. I no longer carry it with me at all times. What a relief! I finally do get to "think of a rose."

Two Teachable Mothers

As a part of my attempt to dispel some of the ignorance that accompanies abuse, I dared to volunteer my time in teaching classes at the public library. The local newspaper supported my idea with an article entitled, *Self Awareness Sessions Help Traumatized People.* And who hasn't been traumatized? Any form of trauma: accidents, divorce or illness can have a negative impact on our lives. Included in the article was a little blurb about my abuse history, and that was what caught the attention of two curious women I will refer to as Mabel and Beth. After the first class, they admitted their daughters were molested. Mabel was especially heartbroken because she had been aware of her husband's sexual abuse. My heart went out to her as she explained, "My daughter is in counseling in a neighboring town. She refuses to have anything to do with me."

"Are you still with your husband?" I questioned, already sensing the answer.

"Yes," she replied. "What can I do?"

I could not help feeling fortunate my grandfather was dead and buried. What should I say to Mable? Basically, I encouraged her to keep coming to the classes, to learn what she could, and to let her daughter know she was gaining understanding. Respecting her daughter's space was essential. Continuing to send little notes and remaining close to her other daughters might be helpful as well. I also suggested she obtain counseling with her husband. We could hope her daughter's therapist would be effective in working with her in this difficult situation.

The two teachable mothers attended every class and were my star pupils. They learned to see themselves and others as treasures, how to decrease worrying and how to view their past with perspective.

I gave Mabel and Beth big hugs at the end of each class they faithfully attended. I admired their courage in standing by their daughters once they revealed their abuse. It took patience to wait hopefully as their daughters attempted to heal. I love Mabel and Beth.

Hints for Mothers of Children with CSA

Following are a few suggestions my mother and I found helpful:

- **Acknowledge**
  If you cannot believe what your daughter is telling you about her past abuse, at least acknowledge the possibility. Comments such as, "I know this goes on," or "I'm shocked, but I will listen," are helpful. The two of you may go on a detective search into her past like my mom and I initially did, seeking information on the possible perpetrator(s). If you are aware of her past trauma and can acknowledge it, your validation can make a huge difference.

- **Apologize**
  My mother did a very comforting thing one day. She called me to let me know that if she had known, she would have done something, anything to help. I believe her. She also apologized for being unaware of the abuse and expressed sorrow for what happened to me.

- **Dare to cry**
  Mother was raised with the belief that crying is a sign of weakness. A most tender moment with her was when she dared to cry with me, to grieve for a bit of her forgotten childhood, and to let the long forbidden tears flow. As she cried, I felt I was loving her four-year-old self. She was the little girl who felt ugly and unwanted and who had decided to be brave and strong and in control by not crying. No wonder she had been unable to cry with me. She blurted out great pain and sorrow and it was a privilege to be there for her. She no doubt thought it was embarrassing that night the way she cried in my arms. I respected that and the following morning when she said "goodbye" at the airport, there was nothing mentioned of her wonderfully human and vulnerable moments the night before.

- **Offer a positive outlook**
  With your daughter's initial disclosure, how can you be positive about what seems to be very negative information? When the

abuse memories surface they can either further haunt her life or give her clues to a more fulfilling and happy life than she has ever experienced. With this understanding, you can give her encouragement. Continue to offer your love.

- **Attend therapy session(s)**
  I appreciated so much my mother's willingness to travel an extra distance to attend a therapy appointment with me. Mothers can be key players in recovery work. Whether consciously aware of the abuse or not, they remain a vital force in the process. I also deeply respect the mothers who seek individual counseling on their own. It is never too late to learn from our past and to make improvements. A friend of mine commented after the death of her parent, "Dad's finally getting therapy!"

- **Pay attention to your spiritual strengths**
  Beware of becoming bogged down with feelings of guilt and inadequacy. This is a good time to strengthen your beliefs about God and His love. Aligning yourself with spiritual truths and requesting divine assistance will make a difference for you and your daughter. I have watched my own mother grow spiritually through the trials I have shared with her. It is as if we are closer to speaking the same language. Your spiritual strength, fed by the Master, will be a blessing to your daughter. Ideas and answers will come to improve your relationship.

I have seen and heard of abuse issues tearing families apart. I am also aware some family members come together after years of distance and misunderstanding. In one of my favorite classes taught by Mr. Robert McDonald, a woman raised her hand to ask, "Robert, is it possible . . .?"

"Yes," he replied, "anything is possible. Next question."

There was a pause, then laughter. He had made his point and in doing so challenged us to examine our thinking. Who are we to set limits on possibilities? Past frustrations, fears and doubts may threaten the mother-daughter relationship, but we must leave that door open. Anything is possible.

"Never Again"

The following story is the experience of a co-worker of mine–a once abused mother who discovered her own child's abuse. In her own words she contributes:

The worst experience of my life was the day that I discovered that my best friend's teenager had sexually abused my own little three-year-old son. At first I did not believe him when he told me, "I don't want to go to his house. He hurt me out in their woods. I don't wanna go there, never, never again!" After confronting my friend, she talked with her son and sadly confirmed the truth with the promise she would get her son into therapy. We both cried together. I called Child Protective Services and also had a police officer come visit us to make a report of the crime. He offered consolation and assured my son that what happened was not his fault.

Unwilling to read one more chart about our patients' histories of child abuse, I quit my job and determined to find more joy in life. His play therapy, as I observed from behind the one-way mirror, was healing for myself as well as for him. I wondered what my life would have been like if I would have had such an opportunity to receive treatment for my mistreatment. I was grateful my boy talked and was also upset with myself for not teaching him how to protect himself from forceful unwanted behavior. I lost my best friend and my job but gained a happier son and a healthier outlook.

CHAPTER 14

To Fathers

"Always Call Me Daddy"

From my reading, I have gleaned that father-daughter incest accounts for 90 percent of reported cases of child sexual abuse, and the natural assumption is that the father (or stepfather) is the guilty party. For a long time following my first major flashback, I believed, along with my therapists, that my father was the primary perpetrator. I then surmised from Grandma's disclosure (with her insistence "You can't blame a dead man–and it happened so long ago.") that my grandfather was guilty of the brutal attack. However, my father and I have never had a healthy father-daughter relationship. When I asked him if he believed his father abused me as a child, he remarked, "That is not the question. I would defend him and forgive him." His attitude is that it is not necessary to speak about CSA. "Let into your mind only the things you want to be there" is his advice. He did not understand that is exactly what I had done–in the past. It had required all of my energy and strength. It wasn't an option. The knowledge had burst through the dam, and I could no longer contain it. I could only let it out and learn to deal with it in small increments.

For several years following my first major flashback, I had little desire to see my father who had seemed unsupportive of my situation.

It was no secret that my father wanted a son. His European upbringing had convinced him a son made a man manlier–and I was his second daughter. He was committed to his military career and was often away from home. Mom, her parents, and his mother were my main caregivers. Fathers in my day were less involved in the parenting role compared with today's dads and I have little memory of his participation in my upbringing. I do remember trying my best to impress him with good table manners. His cars were very important to him. Sometimes I felt jealous of the attention they received. To this day, I do not highly value vehicles. As a four-year-old little girl, my daddy was my hero. He was handsome like a movie star. People used to say he looked like Paul Newman and I wanted to be very pretty so people would know I was his daughter. I remember the day I realized he was leaving us. My parents were divorcing. I have no memory of them fighting. I had seen my mother cry only one time. She had thrown herself across her bed and was sobbing. In my childish mind, I guessed that my daddy was dead. "It's worse than that!" she confessed. Yes, matters were serious and he was saying "goodbye" to me on our front porch. Due to the divorce and the impending move, I surmised that I was losing my father. I asked if he wanted me to call him by his given name or by his nickname. "Always call me Daddy," he had replied.

Abandoned

It felt awful to move away from him to another state where we would live closer to grandparents. I carried his picture with me everywhere. I cried bitter tears when my girlfriends' fathers were attentive to them and when I saw fathers in movies tenderly caring for their daughters.

When my dad visited, I would try so hard to impress him. He would buy my sisters and me expensive Christmas gifts and take us to dinner. I never could get enough food, clothing or attention from him. We traveled to visit him each summer for a week, but he seemed preoccupied and aloof. I would return feeling starved, never having received the secure relationship for which I longed. I would leave a part of my heart at the end of each visit. I remember how we stood atop a hill as I tearfully told him how unfair it was that he could not be our dad. I was always trying to get him to show emotion. That night, overlooking the city, he explained he had no feelings. He simply did not know how to relate to me as a daughter. There were times when I felt more like his girlfriend than his daughter, and I continued in my efforts to appear clever, intelligent and as attractive as my plain features would allow.

As a teenager, I had enough lack of confidence without the added confusion of his visits. One year during his annual Christmas visit I even became ill and refused to see him altogether. I developed a terrible stomachache. He had a poor tolerance for sickness, so it was the perfect excuse.

Strained Relationship

Yearly birthday calls and lovely Christmas presents were the only ties I had with my father. Even after my marriage, a huge gap existed where his love needed to be. After the delivery of my second son, I hobbled to the hall phone and called Dad. His only reaction to my announcement was, "You'll make a good Den Mother." Wondering why I called him, I returned to my room with the familiar longing for sincere caring.

Twenty years later, my relationship with my father was still strained. I felt prompted one day to call my father. It was not his birthday (my usual reason to call) and I was reluctant to place the call. I surprised him and myself as I said, "I just want you to know you make me ill, literally. The reason I refused to be with you at times as a teenager was that I was ill. My stomach always ached. I wanted to feel like your daughter and not your girlfriend." Then I asked him to keep his distance in the future. I did not even want his arm around me and he was to refrain from calling me, "Baby": He agreed. We had our first honest talk, conversing for over an hour, while I sat on the cold basement stair of our farmhouse, guaranteeing privacy. He was surprisingly receptive. He had been reading a psychology book a friend of his had written and admitted I had not received proper attention and affection. Never having revealed this information before, he shared with me his own childhood pain where he experienced a lack of natural affection. He emphasized that he could imagine how hard it must be for me. It was a good thing that I made that call. It prepared us both for the visit to follow a few months later.

In 1984, my sisters and I traveled to Dad's home state to attend the funeral of our aunt (his sister). He kept his word. No physical contact; he even made a point of sitting on the opposite side of the couch from me. No stomachache. He respected the boundaries I had set with him.

My sisters and I sang together at the funeral. He cried as he attempted to deliver his speech and although he was terribly embarrassed, he became more human in my eyes.

With the first major flashback, I tried desperately to find the facts. I knew I had been abused and who should be better able to give me assistance in discovering the culprit(s) than my parents? I needed to find out who had been the perpetrator in my first flashback. In fact, none of my flashbacks revealed perpetrators, only the emotions and pain.

Dad was silent when I explained to him over the phone about my recent return to childhood terror. I felt as though he minimized, even ignored, the trauma I felt. He had nothing to say and no help to offer. It was hard for me to believe he would not be more shocked, or at least have questions over what I was conveying to him. It felt like he would rather believe I was exaggerating, creating the story, or even crazy, than for him to accept any part of my experience as truth. I told him I had never had a childhood and how, after recalling the abuse, I felt free to have fun. (This was the day my son and I had ridden go-carts, when I had so much fun.) Later, describing the encounter with my father to my mother, she said that he was always quiet when questioned and that was just his personality. Nevertheless, my daddy-daughter relationship had never been secure. It did not offer me a parent I could turn to or protection from Grandpa. My father was unwilling to help me with the abuse picture, but, as I noted earlier, he was willing to help buy a go-cart. The next morning he called.

"Vic, I need more information. You did not give me any details."

I broke out into a sweat, thinking, "How can I tell him the embarrassing details of my flashback and the specific content of recent therapy?"

"I need to know," he continued, "the size of the go-cart, and the price."

Acceptance

I suppose I grew tired of the process, the wondering and the waiting. With the passage of time, the issues no longer were who betrayed me and what exactly happened to me as a child. They were replaced with, "How do I live more fully from here on?" Something from within my being had become satisfied. I had gathered enough facts and it was all right. Every one of us knows how frustrating it is to be split, with one part of us wanting one thing and another part of us wanting another. A large part of me had cried and searched and was frightened and desperate to be heard. My inner self had listened to and validated that part. It had matured to a point of settling, as if a negotiation had taken place with the other parts within me. I know what I know, and it is only for me to know. I feel whole and at peace with the integration that took place. Remember, this process took years to accomplish.

Dad continued to call each year on my birthday. I had moved across the United States. I felt I had little need for a father until I had a life-threatening health crisis. I called him and shared my concern, plus the fact that I was not prepared to die until the book I was writing was finished. I even told him the subject matter and he remarked to my surprise, "If writing this book gives you the will to live, then write it."

Apparently, I must have felt I needed his permission to write this book. I did feel better about it after the conversation. It was also evident I still wanted his approval. I believe his giving me permission to write the book was, in a way, a substitute for saying I was okay.

Glimpses of My Father

In reading about Malachi's proclamation at the end of the Bible, which stresses the necessity of turning our hearts to our fathers, (Malachi 4:6), I determined it was time to see my father, and I encouraged his visit. I informed him by phone that his mother had pretty much admitted that Grandpa was the one who brutally abused me when I was three years old. Two weeks later, upon opening my front door, I greeted my father, whom I had not seen for five years. There stood a well-dressed, elderly gentleman with a wide smile, bent a bit with age, yet still handsome. He was a positive and enthusiastic guest, often expressing appreciation for the countryside and our nice home. As we said "goodbye" at the airport, he put his arm around me and said quietly into my ear, "I love you, Baby."

"Whatever," I replied flatly, shaking my head.

My sisters and I sang with our dad at Grandma's funeral. It was during one of our many song practices I requested we have a prayer for our struggling efforts. "I can do that!" he volunteered. We knelt together behind the pew and he offered a sweet prayer. I looked at him from the corner of my eye to check if I was dreaming. It had always been my dream to have such a concerned and sensitive father-one that would pray with me.

During four months of serious financial crunch, my father provided monthly support checks and frequent calls. He seemed to take a regular interest in my well-being and that of my family I have never felt more cared for by my father. Although we were financially strapped, the healing that occurred was tremendously freeing. As we recovered our earning capacity, his phone calls dwindled. My expectations returned to minimal; just the yearly birthday phone call with its superficial chat.

I wish I could report that my dad and I have a functioning father-daughter relationship today, but the fact is predictable feelings of neglect still creep into my heart. However, the feelings of dread, excessive neediness, and anxiety are gone and that's progress.

"Thank you for Crying"

My Stepfather's Reaction to My Abuse Disclosure

Right up there with fathers as the most likely to be the abuser in a girl's life, I found statistics identifying stepfathers.

In my case, my stepfather is completely innocent in the area of sexual abuse and I pay tribute to him for that. Unfortunately, we did not have a satisfying close relationship either. I was seven years old when Mom remarried, and he naturally bonded with my younger sister. I did not fit into his picture of a well-ordered life. It seemed I often got in his way by talking during his favorite TV shows. Through his eyes, I was non-compliant with family rules. His discipline methods seemed punitive to me. I remember him grounding me for simply leaving bobby pins on the floor. My stepfather deserves credit for his strength during my troublesome fourteenth year. He is the one who helped me conquer my school phobia by taking me to school in spite of my balking. I am grateful he had the determination to follow through with the doctor's order. Without it, I could have remained in my room all these years!

Time is healing some of our differences. I love to visit his well-cared-for garden and wish he had shared his green thumb with me. One of my treasures is a tape of him singing his childhood songs.

Following the news of my abuse recall, he talked to me on the phone. It was obvious he was crying. Although my information was sketchy in the beginning, he had evidently believed mother when she shared with him my trauma. He told me, "We love you, honey. Now, you hang in there and remember that!" He knew exactly the right words to say at the right moment and he dared to speak them with great emotion.

Suggestions for Fathers

- **Be aware of emotional incest**
  Remember your role as protector, but do not overdo it to the point that your daughter feels she belongs to you only or that you must have complete control over her. It is burdensome for a young girl to believe she is the number one person in her father's life. *Emotional Incest,* by Dr. Patricia Love and Jo Robinson, could be useful for fathers in helping them to understand what it means and how to avoid it.

- **Meet your main needs for validation and affection with your partner**.
  Your daughter will thrive from your good example. There are sexual and non-sexual ways to relate to her. Romanticized relationships with children are unhealthy. Listen to her if anything you are doing is making her uncomfortable. It took me 39 years to assert myself. Many children today are more expressive, which can be good. Love and respect bind healthy relationships. Give her fatherly hugs with regular reminders that you love her

CHAPTER 15

Sisters, Sisters
There Were Never
More Devoted Sisters

Some of you may remember that wonderful song about the sisters who were so devoted to one another. My two sisters and I have sung it together, even adding our own version to further personalize it. In truth, my sisters have lived up to this descriptive title. As the words indicate, "Through all kinds of weather, we stick together!" Not having had a brother, I am including my sisters in this family section as examples of sibling support.

Many of the readers may not enjoy a close relationship with their siblings and abuse issues may have distanced them even further. I have heard many people explain how the family became divided into two camps: those who know and got therapy and those who remained indifferent or aggressively opposed to opening the possibility of family history gone askew. I have also learned that in some cases one's own discovery of abuse may trigger a sibling's memories of abuse. Also, in some families, as in my situation, only one daughter is molested. This means the other siblings are not able to relate to the experience or to identify with the results of having such a background. I have witnessed examples where the abused sister is hurt and confused at being singled out, causing bad feelings toward the others who somehow escaped the trauma. This is especially painful when the other siblings doubt the abuse in the first place.

In offering some direction to siblings of sisters abused, I share with you my own sisters' fine examples:

- **They believed me.**
  Being believed when I described such extreme circumstances of my abuse has been so appreciated. My family labeled me as the one who exaggerated to the point that people frequently would not believe the simplest details I tried to relate. My sisters never doubted the reality of my abuse.

- **They joined with me in my search for clues and answers.**
  We were each searching for truths. They dared to carefully review our past for leads. I often felt like giving up, and they helped me to follow through with necessary work.

- **They listened and made helpful observations.**
  Most of our communication occurred on the telephone across many miles, yet I could feel my sisters with me almost as if they were in the same room. I could tell them anything, day or night. They have actively listened from my first crazy-sounding disclosure, to this present day. From "Woe is me, I'm feeling awful," to "Wow, it's me, I'm feeling great!" they have gallantly traveled this recovery road with me. I have never felt criticism from them. Their communication was open and amazingly objective at those times when I needed an outside opinion.

- **They showed empathy and unconditional love.**
  Having not shared my background, my sisters could not relate to my trials, yet they had the gift of compassion, which upheld me through the tough times. They had a wonderful ability to laugh over the insanity of my predicament. We rejoiced in my victories when I was able to have fun, and we cried together when I felt I would never recover.

- **They were good examples to me.**
  They would often share tender and fun-loving accounts of their experiences that would touch my soul in such a way that I adopted them as models. We took turns teaching and then learning from one another.

- **They helped teach our parents.**
  After all, we were from a different generation than our parents. My parents had questions, too, and often turned to my sisters for insight. They admitted feeling ignorant on the subject of sexual abuse and complained that reading books the therapist recommended was not helping enough.

To my dear sisters I am forever grateful. There were never such devoted sisters! Thank you. As the song indicates, I appreciate that we have stuck together through all kinds of weather.

CHAPTER 16

To Children

"Lullaby and Goodnight, Thy Mother's Delight"

When my first son was born, I memorized this familiar lullaby. The second verse was my favorite: "Sweet visions untold, thy soul shall unfold. God will keep thee from harm, thou shalt wake in my arms." Over the years, I sang it to each of my babies as I lovingly rocked them to sleep.

One of my counselors thoroughly believed it was no coincidence that God gave me six males to raise, as if He knew I needed to make peace with the other sex. My six sons are some of the finest men I have ever had the privilege to know. Having a mom loaded with emotional issues has been hard on them, I am sure. It is no secret that a hidden history of sexual abuse can produce some seemingly crazy reactions. The bulk of my story has not been open to my children until written on these pages. Because of the subject matter, this book is understandably troubling to them. Hopefully, it will provide insight for them and for others whose mothers, sisters, girlfriends, or wives may have been abused. When dealing with the onslaught of painful memories, it is difficult to be thrust back and forth from the emotions and reactions of a child into the reality of motherhood. One minute I would be in the past and then, ZAP, I would be in the present. Fortunately, for my children's sake, I was home alone during my first major flashback when I had no awareness of being a wife or mom.

There were some days when it was especially rough, like the time I returned from a very difficult and revealing therapy session, vomiting until I was exhausted. I packed my aching head in ice and was in a very sorry state. The hours passed slowly in my dimly lit bedroom. I remember sitting up in bed, propped up with pillows and an ice bag on my throbbing head, when my 19-year-old son entered the room. A vessel in my eye had ruptured from the dry heaves and I must have looked horrid. He held me in his arms, having no way of understanding what I was experiencing. I was speechless due to exhaustion. Many years prior I had held this son as an infant in my arms and had sung to him, "Thou shalt wake in my arms." Now the roles reversed as I allowed myself to lean into the safety of *his* arms. I will always be grateful for his comfort during my second most distressing flashback. He did not have an awareness of the cause for my trauma. He was just there. Perhaps this was God's way of offering personal assurance and warmth.

Rage of the Abused

There were times when I would be full of rage. I would run out of our farmhouse and head for the barn where I would sob into the bales of hay. No one could say or do anything to help me. I would beg to be alone–then sink into desperate loneliness. Following a disagreement with my husband one evening, I remember curling up on the floor of the back seat of our car, trying to disappear. I was stunned that I would have such a reaction–such a powerful form of regression. I had reverted to being a helpless child. These experiences gave me glimpses into Little Victoria, and I learned to respect them.

Then there was the day I was demonstrating to my sons how to release anger (as opposed to fighting with one another). I hit a pillow on the bed shouting a word with each punch such as "angry," "fighting," "trouble," "pain." Before I knew what was happening, I was the one pounding that poor pillow and shouting words until I was exhausted. It had turned into my outlet instead of theirs. I had not realized I possessed rage to that degree. The boys did not feel like fighting any more, but my behavior terrified them. As a result, I learned the importance of getting away when I felt I was about to burst with emotion. Luckily, we had a dump for foliage debris nearby. I would get into the car and drive slowly and carefully down into it. It seemed entirely fitting, since I felt down-in-the-dumps anyway! There I let it all out with sobs of despair that revealed amazing truths. Usually, I would return feeling much better, but on one occasion, I had actually injured my vocal cords and had to refrain from even whispering for a week! This was quite amusing to my family. We all laughed about how quiet our household had become. Eventually the outbursts decreased in intensity and number.

Home Lab

With the knowledge of my abuse came a certain strength I had not known; the power of feeling validated, of believing in myself and my perceptions and the courage to speak up for what I believe. When my victimized self came to the surface–"Poor me, I am helpless. My life is out of control."–I then realized I could stand up for myself and take action. I did a lot of experimenting with assertiveness and the effects of my changing reality had impact on the lives of my sons. I love the saying, "Our homes are the laboratories where we do experiments." I had numerous opportunities to practice. Just as in my chemistry lab, some yields were zero and some were surprisingly successful!

My children have taught me how to have fun, be silly, ride a go-cart, tolerate noise and confusion, love music, climb mountains, rappel over cliffs, work harder, make my dreams happen, stand for my beliefs, to "go for it," "mellow out," eat heartily and to love nature. They have had to deal with a mother's metamorphoses. Their mom has changed with the evolution of her abuse recovery cycle. How different my influence on them would have been had I remained depressed and frightened. I believe they are able to experience greater freedom, sense of identity and purpose in this life as a direct result of my work.

On Becoming Real

Having an abuse background provides many opportunities to become real. I value the term "real" as referred to in the *Velveteen Rabbit,* by Margery Williams. I remember reading this book to my boys as they sat perched on the window seat in our farmhouse. Tears were streaming down my face as I read about the Skin Horse's reply to the Velveteen Rabbit's question about how long it takes to become "Real." It really is a process that takes a long time. The story describes how the transformation doesn't happen to people who are fragile and that you can have some unpleasant physical changes in the process. Of course, rabbit wanted to be "Real" without the accompanying losses.

I had a friend tell me once, "I want to be more like you, but I don't want to have to go through what you have gone through to get there." Remember, part of becoming real is being loved. My opportunities have been many. Like the Velveteen Rabbit, much of the process has been difficult for me. My eyes have not dropped out yet, but some wear and tear is obvious. My trials have given me opportunities. I also have had a great deal of love. When my boys say in jest, "Get real, Mom," I smile.

CHAPTER 17

Grandmothers

"It Only Happened Once"

A letter to my father's mother:

Dear Grandma,

I did not dare publish this book while you were alive because of the fear it would kill you. You were so frail at 93 and easily upset. Besides, you had told me several times to just forget about what happened to me and to stop talking about it. When I originally questioned you about my initial flashback, your response was emphatic, "Nothing bad could have happened to you. Your mother kept you so cute and clean." No words from my mouth ever so completely unnerved you as those spoken on the topic of my abuse. I realized you did not want to help me in my search for facts.

My life had been so enmeshed in yours, I often felt I belonged more to you than my own mother. Dad helped me identify the initial source of this attachment when he told me of your proclamation at the time of my birth, "This one is mine!" Evidently, with my older sister's birth, my mother's mother claimed her to be theirs. She began with and retained the status as the favorite of that side of the family. Thus, when I was born you felt it was only fair that I be dubbed "yours". My dependency on you for validation, financial resources and almost for life itself was keenly felt until I understood and accepted the family dynamics and situation of my abuse. Whenever I was troubled, you were there for me. I always knew you were my emotional and financial backup, until the day you phoned and angrily told me there would be no more money. If I needed help, I should go to someone else. You had heard of my quest to determine who had abused me and that I was wondering if it could have been my dad, your son. This was the one and only time you ever lost your patience and actually yelled at me. The conversation was long and heated. I was taking notes I have saved to this day as final evidence to myself that I did not imagine my abuse. I thank you for that witness. I wrote word for word what you said, and that documentation is important to me. It is my witness that I did not make up the story. Your words were revealing: "I've had hard times too, but I go on. I know it happens. Can't you just bury it? You shouldn't say such things! Well, it happened so long ago, why talk about it now? You said horrible things. This is your way of getting even with your dad for leaving your mother. You got the idea from working with people like you do. Stop talking! I can't listen any more. Yes, I believe it happened to you. It only happened once, and it was not your dad. He is good and kind. You're alone on this one!"

What you did not know is that at the conclusion of the call, I suffered a great decline in my health. I staggered to the couch and lay there in a tightened ball, knees drawn up and fists clenched to my chest, head bent with taut neck muscles. I remained all night in this position. I had talked about my abuse and the worst had happened. I was cut off from what I considered my life source. Upon awakening the next morning, I realized something was physically wrong with me, as well as emotionally. I would later find out I had a birth defect in my brain stem causing pressure against the spinal cord.

It saddened me that our relationship was adversely affected for several months. My dependency shifted to my husband, where it needed to be all along and even shifted to myself to a greater degree. I wondered what it would be like when we traveled to visit you the following summer. Do you remember that visit, when we perched upon the familiar kitchen stools and chatted away as if time didn't matter? I was laughing about how much I liked to dust at your house because I did not have to move anything. You told me to just dust around things. I loved how imperfect it was. You took hold of my hand and kissed my fingers crying, "Victoria, my dear little Victoria!" and I knew we had healed. Our relationship would never be the same; it would be better. I could be independent of you. I felt I could survive your death. I vowed to take care of you, a healthy reversal of roles. And, Nana, how fortunate I was to be able to be with you during your last days on earth. Although you were in a coma, I was right by your side singing, reading and praying. I figured you would understand my feeble attempts to comfort you.

You lingered in that comatose state while miracles happened in the hospital room. Perhaps you were waiting to die until my father and I recognized each other in the roles where we belonged. In that humble room, Dad saw me, I think, for the first time. I was weary and he expressed appreciation for my ability to care for his mother when he felt so helpless. He showed me more compassion and tenderness than I had ever known from him.

I realize you had thought it best to keep silent at all costs, but I had to know, dear Nana, and you were my only witness. I truly believe you thought your love and indulgence would keep me safe. Instead, I was left groping in a maze of confusion. You were a key player in my drama. You are my grandma and I like to imagine in your heavenly state, you now understand why I needed to talk and to write. Nana, I will always love you.

Victoria

"Grandma is Having to Take Extra Nerve Pills"

A letter to my mother's mother:

Dear Grandma,

When mother told me you were having to take additional "nerve pills" because I was talking about what happened to me as a little girl, I really felt sorry for the pain I had caused you. Then I stood back and asked myself, "Wait a minute. I didn't cause the abuse." It was not my fault I was abused. I know you suffered with me because you loved me and that added to my distress. Actually, you suffered through all of my growing up knowing I was unhappy and sick too much of the time. None of us were adequately cushioned for the shock of discovering the cause.

I remember our walk in the park at the family gathering. We talked about how awareness of the abuse had shed light on my childhood concerns. I used to enjoy hearing about when I stayed overnight with you and how I would not go to sleep. You told me you would say, "Now, Victoria, close those big brown eyes of yours and go to sleep." We have laughed at my response for years, "My mommy (s)ay my eyes ope!" We discussed how I had good reason to keep my big brown eyes open as long as possible and that neither bubble baths nor Grandpa's story reading with me cuddled on his lap could relax my guard or protect me from frequent nightmares. Your husband never hurt me and yet my symptoms likely overlapped onto my visits with you and Grandpa.

During my teen year of school phobia, you tended me while Mom worked. No matter how delicious your cooking or how warm your caring, I was frightened, depressed and had little appetite. You knew something was wrong with me and now, in light of the abuse revelation, my explanation of the fears and phobias made sense. Most touching to me on our walk that day was when you cried, "I'm sorry, Victoria. You were such a miserable little thing. I did not know why you were so unhappy. I was so hard on you. I am sorry for all the times I spanked you. I didn't know."

Thank you for believing me, Grandma. You needed my reassurance and comfort as much or more than I needed yours. The walk was good.

The following day you informed me that you really could not believe me. I knelt down to look up into your eyes, taking hold of your little hands. "It's okay, Grandma, if you don't believe me. It's hard for me to believe me and I'm the one it happened to. But I must believe. It's all right if you don't." It felt strange to be supporting you, Grandma, when I was so in need of the comfort you had given one day earlier.

When I realized I needed additional therapy for treatment of depression following my surgery, I prayed I would somehow find the financial support required for me to fly to the treatment center in Denver. It was difficult to feel I was worth the time and money involved. I was surprised when Mom called to say, "Grandma wants to pay for your tickets to Denver. She wants you to be happy." Hooray for you, Grandma! I am grateful you lived long enough to see the results of my treatments.

Thank you Grandma, for your hugs, scrumptious homemade foods and for the hundreds of times you said to me, "Bless your little heart." I will always love you.

Victoria

Suggestions for Grandparents of CSA Victims

Never underestimate the important role you can have in the recovery process of a grandchild. You have a great deal to contribute!

- **Abundant Acceptance**
  You may feel unable to accept the information about your grandchild's abuse. You might be unable and indeed, even unwilling (especially initially) to accept what she believes happened. However, you can accept her need to search for the facts, as you are part of her history. This is not about you; it is about her. She is attempting to break the silence and may do so with such energy that it feels exhausting and frustrating to you. She will likely make mistakes in saying too much or by withdrawing in frustration. Accept her stages of recovery. Accept her as your granddaughter who has every opportunity for growth and discovery, rather than as a permanent victim of abuse.

- **Selective Support**
  Therapy is expensive even in short-term segments. The emotional burden your granddaughter is experiencing is

tremendous enough without the additional financial burden. Supportive counseling can prevent long-term expenses. If there is a feasible way to assist with some of the expenses, this can be money well spent! Effective treatment can benefit your great grandchildren as well, and their mom can become who she is entitled to be–a healthier, happier being.

- **Lots of Love**
  These tips for grandparents are not numbered in order of importance. Love is so needed and most of us can improve our capacity to love. I challenge you to find ways that will be most suitable for your granddaughter's situation. It may mean regular phone calls, many more hugs and an increased capacity for listening from the heart.

- **Many Memories**
  Hopefully, you have a wealth of information as grandparents, complete with pictures that may be helpful in reminding your grandchild of the good times. There is a tendency among those of us who were abused to have little recall of the bad or the good in our past. And it wasn't ALL bad! For many years, I focused on the negative happenings–and then I learned of the good times. Memories of those times returned often with the help of loved ones and I continue to welcome any tidbits that tell me good things about my childhood. This is an opportunity for you. You may even wish to write her story as my mother did for me–a great treasure of memories to cherish.

CHAPTER 18

Perpetrator

Where Does He Belong?

While organizing my files into chapters for this book, I was wondering where to put the 'perpetrator' chapter. I had written letters to each of my grandparents for the family section, and then I withdrew the letter to my grandfather, my perpetrator. Where did it belong? Certainly not in the family section! Yet, he is a family member, a chilling reminder that our perpetrators are most often members of our own family. Incest is a family affair. Tragically, his behavior and his choices determined his label. In one of the group training seminars I attended, it was emphasized if we tried to put all the victims together, distanced from their perpetrators, we would actually all end up together, because perpetrators usually are untreated victims.

No Black Hats

When I was three, television was very new. In the weekly show "Hopalong Cassidy", I could always count on the bad guy wearing a black hat and the good guy wearing a white one. It gave me a reassuring sense of discernment. Although I never really liked being around my grandpa, he did not wear a black hat. He did not have an evil look on his face. I had no way of seeing the enemy as measured by my TV models.

While touring a state mental institution as a student nurse, I walked with my colleagues through a unit for the criminally insane. With a childhood belief system in place, I continued to hope the convicted murderers would look like murderers. They did not. Some men were a bit sad looking, but they were as normal looking as anyone you would pass without notice on the street. Did I expect to see snarling maniacs in chains? No, but it would have helped if at least they had glared maliciously from beneath the rim of a black hat!

During my public health nursing training, I was given an opportunity to assist in a little boy's child abuse case that resulted in his removal from the home. Those home visits were grueling and confusing. In addition to my awareness of his extreme mistreatment came the realization that the attractive clean home had been a cover for the suspected abuse. His mother kept her children clean and well-dressed.

Let me remind you of Grandma's initial response when I asked her about my abuse: "Nothing bad could have happened to you. Your mother kept you so cute and clean." Grandma held on to her image of me as she wished it to be, refusing to see her husband as a child molester.

It is difficult, if not impossible, to identify a perpetrator. Most of us, including myself, do not have a clue as to which persons are perpetrators because do not have a recognizable identity. They can be charming, affluent and well liked in their communities and churches. It is likely that many perpetrators go through life unrecognized, unreported and unaware what they are doing is seriously wrong!

Because I have worked hard to feel, express and release my anger, the following letter to my grandfather is not full of the rage I have known. It is simply that which I would express to him today if he were alive. Addressing the perpetrator can be a healing process.

Letter to Grandpa

Grandpa,

Grandma told me, "You can't blame a dead man!" when I asked her to please confirm that, indeed, you were the man who sexually assaulted me as a three-year-old. She had insisted, "It happened only once, and it was not your father and besides, it was so long ago." She did not realize she had indeed confirmed that you were the perpetrator. And she was wrong–I could blame a dead man. For I do hold you responsible for what happened to me.

This is not a hate letter, nor is it one of love. It is a letter of acceptance. I have accepted the gross crime that was committed against me as a child. I have accepted the fact that you were the perpetrator. In your behalf, I firmly believe you were not aware of the broad negative impact your actions would have on my future. In your day, nothing was spoken or written on the topic of sexual abuse and its aftermath as it is today. It has been difficult to dilute the mistrust, anxiety, fearfulness and depression I have experienced because of your actions. I have written many letters without mailing them and certainly, you will not receive this one! Yet, it relieves my soul to let you know of my feelings, as well as lack of feelings I have held for you.

Grandma called and asked me to help transport you to the hospital, as you were hallucinating and out of control. In order to get you into the car, I told you we were going to get your blood pressure checked. You believed me and left peaceably. I stayed with you as they admitted you to the lock up facility. As I was saying goodbye, you were telling the staff, "This is my beautiful granddaughter." I walked away without any feeling whatsoever. The staff later told me not to visit until your memory was completely gone. Apparently, you were furious with my deception when you realized you could not leave the hospital. When you died, I was the one who suggested there be no funeral, only a graveside service. When they lowered your casket into the ground, I did not cry.

I must confess I never loved you. I never even liked you. I was afraid of you. I was unimpressed with your fancy Cadillac and financial successes. Avoiding you was my goal, but my desire to be with Grandma meant total avoidance was impossible.

Traveling with Grandma to visit your construction sites was a treat for me. Riding the train, being indulged with coloring books and paper dolls and having anything I wanted to eat, made the trips exciting. I did not like the exposure to your crude comments and what I now know were sexual innuendoes. Grandma tried to be protective, but she did not have the know how to keep me safe.

You are likely surprised I know about what you did to me

50 years ago in Wyoming. Following the abuse, I carried the darkest of secrets, sealed with the threat of death. I had understood Grandma's words that my mother would "kill you" to mean that my mother would kill "me". From that night on, I was robbed of my innocence. My health declined. I was nervous and unhappy. Mom wondered what had happened to her fun-loving little girl. That is behind me now. Thanks to counseling and spiritual strength, I have learned to appreciate and even to enjoy life. One of my intentions is to help others who are afflicted as I have been. Sharing this story may help.

I realize you came from tough European stock and that childrearing methods were harsh in your day. I have been told you challenged your parents and your stubbornness was difficult for them. You seemed to be the proverbial black sheep of the family due to some of the choices you made. You obviously were a successful businessman, as you provided well for your family and had a reputation for being a hard worker. Dad has told me you got jobs during the depression when so many were unemployed. I remember that you were into health foods, and you liked having quotations to hand out to others. You saved money and gave us silver dollars regularly. I'm grateful Mother told me about a time when you apologized to her with tears in your eyes.

While taking a class on changing how our personal history affects us, we were told to visualize our parents' parents, then walk back on a timeline as if observing that grandparent's past from their perspective. For the first time, as I viewed the time of your birth and your challenges, I felt a great surge of merciful compassion. I believe you had well-meaning parents, but it is possible that you were abused (perhaps without their awareness). You may have suffered with an imbalance that caused your moods to fluctuate. I walked away from that class with improved insight that has given me some peace. I can look at your picture and see you as the handsome soldier Grandma fell for. Who am I to judge? Only you and God know what went amiss for you. I feel mercy toward you–not really love–but mercy is an improvement.

Victoria

CHAPTER 19

To Parents

"Mom, You Can't Throw the Vacuum at Me, That's Abuse!"

The Need to Improve

In order to improve our parenting, we each need to be sensitive to the pain we have caused our children. I once attended a program on child abuse. I was feeling distanced from such a sorrowful topic–I had met and mastered my issues, or so I thought. My level of comfort was about to change. In his opening remarks, the presenter stated that each of us likely has been guilty, in one degree or another, of child abuse. On the extreme end of his parenting chart was sexual abuse. Certainly, I was innocent on that one! He also emphasized the need for us to be more aware of physical and emotional abuse. The presenter added, "If you aren't squirming in your seats and feeling a bit uncomfortable during any of my program, then I will have failed in my delivery of this topic." Admittedly, this was an extreme approach, yet it had a positive effect on me, in that I determined to improve my parenting.

I imagine some readers, like me, have felt responsible in some degree for abusing their children. Nevertheless, it is not unusual for all (or most) parents to abuse children in some way while raising them. There is a multitude of things a good parent may do that could be considered abusive. With a history of abuse, pent up rage increases the likelihood of such occurrences. I realized I did not want to resort to hitting my children; however, one day in utter frustration, I literally threw our vacuum at my son who was a few stair steps below me. He yelled, "Mom, that was child abuse! I know you're mad at me, but you can't throw the vacuum at me!" I had to agree.

My personal definition of child abuse is: parenting without respect. I do not like to use the word *abuse*, as it frequently calls up all kinds of images of cruelty with which we do not want to be associated. However, if the word abuse is too troublesome, we will have to adjust to it. Euphemisms cannot change what abuse is or does. The majority of us, who were sexually abused as children, have stopped the pattern of sexual abuse within our own families. Still, we need to be aware of our susceptibility to various child-rearing behaviors that are not in the best interest of our children. Many of us are hyper-vigilant in attempting to restore healthier relationships. Unfortunately, the fact that we may not be sexually abusive does not preclude the possibility we are abusive in other ways.

As long as we treat children with disrespect in any way, abuse on some level continues, and it is our solemn responsibility to continue to work on improvement. Yes, sexual abuse is the furthermost and most damaging extreme, next to murder. However, each time we put a child down with disgust, slap in anger, cause a child to feel humiliated and unwanted, we, too, are child abusers.

Neglect

Following his remarks on sexual and physical abuse, the presenter had us look at the often-overlooked area of emotional abuse. Emotional abuse always accompanies the first two types of abuse. It can also stand alone in its devastation. Again, there are degrees of emotional abuse. The type that perhaps all of us can identify with is neglect.

Is there a parent anywhere today who has not felt guilty of neglect being either physically or emotionally absent when our children have needed us? It is true that it is impossible to always be an attentive parent. There are times of illness and being away from home, or needing time-outs for ourselves. At times children misinterpret sincere efforts on our part as parents. Nevertheless, with today's busy lifestyles, I believe neglect is an area to examine very closely. Even if we are home all day, it is easy to fall into the too-busy trap. There will always be tasks, phone calls, and other demands that can take away from quality time with our children. Have you ever considered that it is abusive to always be busy? In one of my classes on child rearing, a young mother commented, "My mom put more value on how nice the house looked than on our emotional needs. It seemed we could never do things well enough. Our house looked perfect, but we were miserable. Mom would get so upset, she would yell at us a lot."

To counteract her unhappy background, the young mother moved to the opposite approach. "My children and I will be relaxed and happy in a house that is clean, but looks lived in. When Mom visits, her expression is of great disappointment. I talked to her once about it. I told her that I love her but that I just can't keep a perfect house and be the kind of mom I want to be." Extremes in either direction, ranging from perfectionism to total bedlam, can be damaging. After years of suffering with obsessive-compulsive tendencies, I became too relaxed in the area of neatness and orderliness. Balance is a worthy goal!

Verbal Slams

Have you ever yelled at your child and later wondered how you could have lost control to such an extreme? Referring to our children as troublemakers, jerks, or idiots is always damaging. Name-calling in anger, even when using a person's given name, has a powerful negative effect. You do not even have to call them the actual name. How about, "How many times do I have to tell you?" and its multitude of variations? The implication is clear, "You are STUPID." Your voice will become your child's own demeaning voice as they shout to themselves in their heads the repeated put downs you've given them. Anything that causes our children to see themselves as obstacles in our lives is disrespectful and unloving.

Being overly critical is a form of violence and abuse. This is the easiest pattern to fall into with a steady diet of criticism and correction. There are also children who are raised (or lowered) without natural affection by cold and unfeeling parents. My heart goes out to them and I feel sorry for the parents who have not learned to love and value the little ones entrusted to their care.

During one of my therapy sessions with Ann, I was particularly discouraged over my abuse and the abuse suffered by too many people. "There are so many wicked men out there." I exclaimed. She rephrased my comment with, "There are many who have been mis-taught!" That helped. Although I know, for a fact, there are wicked people out there, I have to agree that ignorance and poor role models contribute to abuse. I determined that one of my life purposes would be to re-teach individuals in an attempt to overcome such profound ignorance in child rearing. I have been given many opportunities.

The Abuse Cycle

> *If the definition of a person equals someone who can perform and obey, there is inequality. From a dominant/submissive relationship will come fear, inadequacy, hostility, resentment, sense of imbalance, rage and jealousy.*
> Virginia Satir

When teaching parenting classes, I inform the audience that whether we like it or not, many of us are part of an abuse cycle that has been perpetuated through generations.

Even having chronic illness can be a part of this cycle. Sexual abuse made me sick as a child, and somatic illness continues to be a concern. One way I need to decrease the impact of abuse is to become as healthy as possible.

I received an unexpected teaching opportunity the day I saw a father jerk his tired, wiggling two-year-old out of a meeting. I followed him into the next room where he had closed the door and was about to vent his frustration on the little guy's rear. Naturally, he was furious over my invasion of his private duty. He said he had to discipline his son and it was none of my business how he did it. I asked him how he was disciplined as a child. "Well, I was beaten," he said, "but at least I knew who was boss and I minded. Kids nowadays need more of this treatment. They are out of hand." Fortunately, this dad became teachable after recovering from his initial fury over my interference.

Perhaps the tide is turning for many families today. From my current as a grandma perspective, it is tremendously rewarding to observe my own married sons father their offspring with tender, devoted attentiveness and affection. I thought of myself as a very good parent, but I honestly did not listen to and play with my children as they do. In general, I often see young fathers with increased ability to be empathetic and respectful, and much more involved in the child raising, nurturing process.

Changing the Abuse Cycle

Your Daddy Loves You

One great example of parental love came as I attended a dinner gathering that was full of children and commotion. The dad had to leave for a meeting. His three-year-old threw herself down and cried, "I wanna go, Daddy. I wanna go!" He bent down and said, "I know it hurts, but you can't go this time." He clasped her up into his arms. "Your daddy loves you." The sobs subsided. "I will read you a story when I get home." Then he just held her, stroking her auburn hair thrust against his chest. Her breathing slowed. Time stopped. I was mesmerized, a happy witness of soul-satisfying love. A few moments later, she squirmed out of his arms and ran off to play with her brothers. With tears in my eyes, I told the man that I had just witnessed one of the most tender father daughter scenes of my life. I thanked him and questioned where he learned such wonderful skills. He revealed that he was raised in a very harsh manner and had to learn to be there for his children, and that it was the most rewarding process of his life.

In the grocery store, not only do the angry parents receive my attention, but also those precious parents who, without yelling, slapping or belittling, understand that their tired, ornery little child has reached his limit and it is time to go home. There is a turning point at which children are more important than a completed grocery list. I commend and frequently compliment parents who demonstrate, under stressful situations, respect for their offspring.

The Spanking Lesson

A friend related one of my favorite examples of a mother's attempt to teach her little boy. She said when their third child was born, she determined she would not use spanking as a method of discipline as she had with the first two children. He was the most pleasant little fellow, radiantly happy and well behaved. One day as she carefully planted petunias along their front path, she stood to rest for a moment. Then she noticed her darling son had been following her, pulling up each flower after she planted it. For the first time in his life, she slapped him on his little butt. He wailed! She felt horrid for breaking her resolve, but felt he at least learned the consequence for ruining her efforts to beautify the yard. The next day she began to replant the flowers. No sooner had she planted the first than he bent down and pulled it out. He then hit his mother! Lesson learned.

If there is one parenting lesson I continue to learn, it is that love and respectful firmness produce miraculous feelings and replications of fairness, justice and mercy. Improve on your parents' parenting. Improve on your *own* parenting. The sooner you deal with your own childhood abuse, the less impact it will have on your children. Child mistreatment produces rage that can seek expression through our children. I can testify there is no more rewarding investment of your time, effort and attention than to turn the tide in your family line.

Notes
    1. Satir, Virginia, Workshop taught in Bellingham, Wa., 1988.

CHAPTER 20

Positive Parenting Ideas

1. *Acknowledge your own treatment as a child, both negative and positive.*

Before we can improve on our own upbringing, it is necessary to face the fact there were some problems. One of the many mistakes I made in looking back into my childhood was to forget the good times. Most of us do have those! It was important for me to realize it wasn't all bad. With abuse in our backgrounds, many of us have blocked out the good, as well as the bad. Mother helped me by writing a history of my early life, including how I ate potato bugs in the sand pile, and how I loved to sing and dance in recitals. Relatives have shared with me precious stories of my childhood, and pictures are useful as proof!

2. *Obtain professional help, if needed.*

Recognize that with an abuse history, you will need to address and correct the tendency to overreact and disrespect your children. It saddens me when well-meaning parents call me for advice, admitting they probably need counseling. Yet, too often, they do not take the first step in finding a qualified counselor, or they do not follow through with consistent appointments. Many fear the process and wonder if it will be worth the money. I tell them that finding a support person who can help them to strengthen their family is the best investment of their dollar. In my own family, my husband and I have recognized the need for some additional assistance in dealing with issues previously handled ineffectively. Understanding can bring relief and renewal. We need to overcome ignorance and be willing to learn to try new methods of relating to others.

3. Increase your parenting education.

Attend some of the inspired programs for improved parenting with positive discussion groups. Select helpful books with teaching examples. *The Power of Positive Parenting, by* Glenn L. Latham is just one of the many excellent books available today. Copies have been given to each of my married sons with children.

4. Where possible, become better partners as a couple in the awesome task of parenting.

During the times I did part time shift work as a nurse, it seemed that my husband and I were also parenting on shifts. He would be the parent when I was at work. I would be the parent while he was gone. The unsettling part was, who would do it when we were both home? It was as if we still took turns instead of parenting together. When we parent together and include the Spirit of the Lord in the partnership, all of us feel the effect. One night, following our family prayer, the power of love was so overwhelming a group hug was not enough. I kissed one side of our 14-year-old's face and my husband the other. Our son yelled, "Hey, you guys!" and squirmed away smiling broadly.

6. Follow the examples of positive role models.

These may be found in your family, community, church, circle of friends, or in your spiritual leaders.

A helpful way to change how you deal with your children is to react as if you are the individual you are modeling (or trying to imitate). A powerful example comes from a class I taught on improving parenting. With the assignment to think of a recent incident in which the parent was ineffective, the class members were asked to relive in their minds the same incident as if going through it with the wisdom and understanding of their model. After class, a middle-aged woman approached me with tear filled eyes to relate her experience with the exercise. She had returned from work to find her home a mess. Dirty dishes cluttered the counters, and school papers littered the living room. She really scolded her girls for being so lazy and inconsiderate. But, then, remembering her class assignment, she reviewed the incident through the eyes of her personal role model, Jesus Christ. Now, with this new perspective, she was able to see two precious daughters before she viewed the mess. She was overwhelmed with love and appreciation for them and for the privilege of being their mom. The resentment of being a single parent was gone. She recognized the need to teach them better habits, but appreciated the respectful perspective.

7. *Set some bedtime limits*

I did not let my children sleep in the same bed with me alone or with my husband. Babies, of course, were exceptions. There were times when tired toddlers fell asleep on our bed and we would carry them into their own before retiring ourselves. During times of illness, I would hold them in my arms until they were asleep and then remain in the room at the bedside. Our boys knew if they had a bad dream or a strong storm was in progress, they had two choices: They could call out and we would come and sit with them, or they could join us in our bedroom with their sleeping bag on the floor. We even had a teenager join us with his sleeping bag once at two in the morning during a horrendous storm.

8. *Spice up your parenting with fun and appropriate humor.*

Many of us with traumatic histories have become such serious people! It took a lot of our attention as children to try to figure things out and stay on guard in our families. After all, things weren't right and life often felt heavy. In my own situation, I never felt I was part of the fun times because I did not feel well. Whatever the cause, my children much prefer a "chilled-out" mother. I have often shared with hospitalized mothers in the mental health unit, some ideas for them to try when they go home on a pass. Children accustomed to a serious, depressed mom will welcome a change! My suggestion is to start with dinnertime.

Caveman Dinner
A favorite is our "Caveman's Dinner." (The theory of the evolution of man is not one of our beliefs, which adds to the

humor of our designated meal!) The idea is to have a meal (preferably of meat, a hunk of bread and large veggies), which we consume without the use of plates or silverware. I serve the food on a big platter in the middle of the table and everyone grabs the grub and eats it with just their hands. It is the exact opposite of the "Manners Dinners" we have on Sunday with china, silver, napkins and the practice of having good manners. Lots of fun!

Eating Tool Mix-up

Another idea is to have the children set the table using kitchen tools rather than the standard knife, fork and spoon. Each person must eat dinner with whatever is set by the plate. We like to have spaghetti or rice, the challenge of peas, and so forth. Try eating with an ice cream scoop or a wire whisk! I love hearing the reports of these mothers' experiments with fun when they return to the mental health unit. Hooray for moms who seriously want to become less serious. It *is* possible.

9. *Use appropriate humor and good-natured joking*

In some people's minds, malicious teasing is funny and makes them appear clever. In my mind, it fits into the abuse picture and represents major disrespect toward children.

Laugh Therapy

During her recovery from cancer, my friend Pam called me regularly for her laugh therapy. I would merely describe some of the happenings of my week on the farm with six boys and we would both be laughing. She recovered, and I discovered life could be really funny when we look for the humor. Since then, I have kept a humor file with clippings and cartoons to remind me to laugh. My sons love it when I send them letters with the latest humor in our lives at home. I recently assembled 20 enlarged photos depicting silly times together as a family into a "Joy Book." Thanks to Pam, I am always looking for laughter to share.

My mother, along with others including myself, has marveled over the great sons I have had a part in rearing. People have witnessed my inconsistent ways, and my struggles with orderliness and time management. For some reason, I believe I was given six outstanding boys with tremendous capacities to learn and to love. I have always said when you combine a mother's innate loving capacity with the Spirit, you can come up with creative, wonderful parental responses that overrule less effective ways. Like every mom, I can look back and wish I had mothered better. Instead, I try to relish each day's opportunity to love and support my children and look forward to many more opportunities to improve. Remember, we will never parent perfectly, but we can come a long way in creating a satisfying relationship with our offspring.

VI

SUPPORTIVE OTHERS

One day, I pictured in my mind a large room in which I stood with individuals who had stood by me during my recovery from childhood sexual abuse.

I saw those who:
    Offered solace
    Listened
    Paid attention
    Cried with me
    Gave counsel
    Reassured
    Comforted

And, in my mind's eye, I was surrounded by those who supported me–the room was filled.

Victoria Lynn

CHAPTER 21

Blue Ribbon Recipients

Those who support women with CSA backgrounds

Upon entering the foyer of a large building on the campus of the University of Washington, I was presented with a yellow ribbon to be worn throughout the VOICES (*see* Voices of Incest Can Emerge Survivors) Seattle Conference. In their handout was the following explanation:

> *"An important symbol of VOICES is the yellow ribbon. Members believe that adults who survived physical and/or sexual abuse or neglect as children are as deserving of yellow ribbons as are the men and women of our armed forces and consular corps who were held hostage in Iran. Indeed, many of those adults were taught how to survive confinement, separation from people who cared about them, abuse and or neglect. The whole country celebrated their survival with yellow ribbons.*
>
> *The child who is victimized by a trusted authority figure is held captive not by foreigners but by her or his own family. And the only resources that a child has to rely on are internal. If you are a victim of child sexual abuse, we applaud your survival and encourage you to wear the yellow ribbon, you deserve it."*

On the last day of the conference, friends of survivors were invited to attend. They were given a blue ribbon to wear, indicating their role as 'survivors of survivors' with the following description:

"We believe that victims of child physical and sexual abuse cannot become full-fledged survivors without a great deal of support and caring from pro-survivors–friends, family members and professionals. Because these people are truly our "best" friends, we believe they deserve blue ribbons that convey top quality and first class.

Thank you for the support you are providing for at least one surviving victim of child sexual or physical abuse. We appreciate your help, energy and efforts!"

I was pleasantly surprised to see many partners wearing blue ribbons. They deserved the recognition. Beginning with friends and concluding with the more specific role of partners, this section is devoted to assisting and appreciating those who stand beside the survivors, the blue ribbon recipients.

CHAPTER 22

Friends

My heart has been deeply touched by the many accounts and personal witnesses I have received from caring friends. As a friend of a survivor, you have been the 'angel unaware' when even unknowingly you have been there at the right time and have offered exactly the right words or the silent hug that has had a healing effect on the afflicted one.

Joan, a blue ribbon friend, related to me that she knew about the childhood sexual abuse problem from her experience of befriending, LaNae, who suffered with obesity. In her attempt to lose weight, LaNae had become aware of her CSA and her subconscious belief that having extra weight would somehow keep her safe from further unwanted attention that could possibly lead to abuse. As her memories returned in flashbacks, Joan was there for her. In fact, at one point in her healing, Joan spent an entire night by LaNae's side, reminding her she was safe and not alone. Joan dared to learn of the trials and triumphs of the abused. LaNae was able to recover and over the years, she lost the additional pounds, as well as the heaviness of spirit that had interfered with her happiness. As a steadfast, trusted friend, Joan was a prime player in her recovery.

A Denver woman I interviewed for this book shared with me her comfort in being held during a crisis in her life:

> *It was like a prayer to me that day. I was sitting there with this woman who held me in her arms, and I cried. This was the only one who ever held me like that and I cried those tears about all that stuff. And it was like this incredible rebirth. Without my telling her, she perceived I thought I was going to die. I experienced a change in myself that day she held me.*

My own priceless friend, Pam, saw me through many of the best and the worst times of my survival work. Her consistent calls were often informative, always empathetic. She never gave up on me. Her history of emotional and physical abuse gave us common ground for commiserating. Within moments of my collapse the week following brain surgery, she appeared at my door along with the paramedics. She had heard the call for help on her husband's scanner. While I was in the throes of my own hellish return to being a helpless, terrified child, Pam talked reassuringly as she packed my necessary items. She even traveled with me to the hospital in a nearby town. Living angels of this caliber can never be forgotten. Such persons are to be commended for their courage and unwavering devotion to those of us who have known intense suffering.

I truly believe a person's abuse issues need to be allowed full expression with each new discovery, and beautiful indeed is the friend who supports her in her journey. First, there is an acceptance of the truths, which will help to free her from a long denied past. As her supportive friend, you may witness many tears from the abused one as the grieving process unfolds. Hopefully, you will eventually also see an increase in her energy and ability to feel joy.

Next, there is her search for finding herself and for learning to love herself unconditionally. As this occurs, her neediness will lessen and a new phase of friendship will begin.

CHAPTER 23

Partners

Oh, the lament of the man who realizes the lady he loves is a survivor of sexual abuse!

"I didn't ask for this!" he exclaims. Neither did she.

"I didn't know she had this kind of background before I married her." is another very common observation–Very often, neither did she. Some women are aware of their past and choose to conceal their powerful secret. And then there are those who, like me, have no idea of their CSA history before entering the relationship. It often emerges at around age 40 and/or following a traumatic event such as childbirth. Whether your partner was compelled or motivated to deal with her childhood sexual abuse history, you have an important role in her recovery. In discussing my book project, many men have expressed their bewilderment concerning their partners with CSA. These choices may be helpful:

1. You can choose to separate from her.

By this, I do not mean physical abandonment. A more preferable way of separating is that in which each becomes a separate individual. Your partner's abuse history is not yours. You do not own her experience, but as her partner, you can assist her recovering from the effects of her history.

Marriage tends to merge us together until we believe our loved one ought to think and act as we do. Becoming separate is tricky but also exciting because at a certain point two healthier individuals come together. Two halves in marriage do not equal a whole person, even though the "math" is correct. Two wholes equal one improved marriage.

There was a time in my marriage when we were struggling with identity and boundaries. We felt we really were not ready for marriage, a shocking discovery when you are already committed! We had been married for four years. My husband leaned over one day in a meeting we were attending and asked, "Will you wait for me?" (Since I had begun resolution of my abuse issues well before he was aware of the abuse in his background, he was asking that I not heal and leave him behind.) With the realization of my CSA, my husband's child abuse (not of the sexual type) came into his awareness. That meant both of us were suffering from the return of painful memories. With each of us receiving therapy we made sacrifices of time and money. We were together in our need to heal separately for a while.

2. You may choose to increase your understanding of the dynamics of childhood sexual abuse.

The woman with CSA issues is often in turmoil. She has the signs, symptoms, perhaps some of the "a-ha" moments that explain many of her reactions. She also has recovery work ahead of her. She brought her past with her into the relationship, and as it comes more fully into her awareness, she may suffer with additional mistrust, nightmares, sleepwalking, night terrors, fears of abandonment, decreased emotional as well as physical (sexual) closeness, depression and illness. Add to this picture a partner who is upset with her discovery and/or disclosure, and the scenario worsens.

You, as a partner, hold a unique position in the support you can offer your companion as you recognize that her seemingly abnormal behavior is a reaction to previous negative experiences. This takes a healthy partner! My husband has been the recipient of my confused thinking on several occasions.

From my own experience, I have some examples of how CSA can challenge a relationship. There was the time during our sleep, when he innocently rolled over, put his arm around my waist, and was met with furious rapid kicks from me that awakened both of us. On another occasion, he merely got out of bed to use the bathroom and upon returning was met with my fury, "Why did you leave me when I needed you so badly?" Evidently, seeing the dim reflection of a man in my bedroom had triggered a flashback. I had felt instant terror and nausea and was paralyzed in fear. Time had stopped. I seemed frozen in that position, not daring to move for a very long time and no one was there for me. Thus, a few moments were to me as hours. My husband could have used such times as evidence that his wife was unloving and somewhat crazy.

I once had a hospitalized patient tell me her husband was tormenting her. She went on to explain, "Sometimes he enters our living room when I am sitting in a chair and he comes in behind me. Suddenly there he is and I get so startled I feel like I'm going to lose it." This young woman was in the process of dealing with her traumatic CSA history. I was able to explain to the husband that such an over reactive startle reflex was triggered by her original problem of never knowing when her perpetrator would surprise her. They were very grateful for the insight. It is never funny or clever to startle another person, particularly one who has a background of CSA. Some husbands continue to challenge the startle reflex with great inconsideration.

3. If you have abuse in your past, you may choose to face your own history with its recovery issues.

You might discover your own mistreatment, as my husband did, as your partner becomes more aware of hers. When each of you comes from an abusive background, the relationship may be strained, distorted, unhappy or avoided altogether. People can live together without having a relationship. They struggle with closeness and often feel lonely and unloved. Each one of us is hungry for love from the moment we are born. Those raised with even a partial diet of disrespect and cruelty, often do not have their love and security needs met, and then they enter marriage with additional hunger to be truly loved. Fortunately, some women do find partners who are capable of offering consistent caring, gentleness and security. More often, however, an abused woman tends to marry a person with a similar background, with similar needs for recovery work.

I hope you are willing to participate in counseling and will find a support system that will be most helpful. With recognition and treatment, you can replace the abuse pattern with a more promising relationship. With your improved example, you will have a positive impact on future generations.

Juanita offered this insight on the relationship theme:

I was talking to someone last week and I said, I am really being careful about relationships now. I try to make sure they do not have any issues. But that's impossible. What I should be looking for is where, in their process, they are. Are they trying to move toward a place of healing and wholeness? If I can find someone whom I can support and who is supporting me, then we can move to that place together. There is going to be a functional relationship, finally. It will be about healing; it will be about trust.

4. If your relationship with your partner has its own history of abusiveness, you may choose to break the pattern of mistreatment and build a more positive foundation.

There are partners who simply feel, "I don't want to go through this with her." You can stay with her but remain aloof, critical, even condemning. This choice compounds the abuse. I think we are all guilty of this choice at times when the situation feels overwhelming.

Your partner must deal first with her past, which demands attention and healing. She next has the challenge of discovering ways to protect herself from further mistreatment. As a friend of mine said about the title, *Dear Sister, Once Abused,* "It tells me the abuse doesn't continue; that it is over and that is comforting." In order to heal, it is important for a survivor to refuse to permit anyone to degrade her. She has a need to surround herself with positive, supportive persons who will respect her. Your partner needs to be accepted just as she is. Affirming her growth along this journey will speed her recovery. Be aware that your marriage can have a perpetrator/victim theme. Each of you can fall into old patterns, some of them modeled after our own parents' patterns. You may be successful in not repeating the type of abuse you experienced as a child (such as sexual abuse or child beating), yet suffer with verbal abuse–both of you giving and receiving the devastating blows. I have found that Suzette Elgin's book, *You Can't Say That To Me!* is very useful in helping to recognize and treat this common problem.

5. *You can choose to use creative ways to enhance your relationship.*

When teaching problem-solving classes, I like to encourage every listener to use the "three C's": courage, curiosity and creativity. I am a great believer in using imagination effectively. At one point in our marriage, twenty-four years ago, we were not getting along well at all. It seemed neither of us could say nor do anything right. My husband was working swing shifts from 3 to 11 p.m. I wrote a letter to him and tucked it into his lunch pail. It went something like this, "I need a friend. Could you meet me at 11:15 tonight at my place? Looking forward to being with you, Victoria." At 11:15, we met in our spare room where we talked as friends for hours. I remember him saying things such as, "Maybe your husband feels this way . . ." It felt good to be listened to and to gain understanding in a non-threatening way–so good we met again the next evening and the next. Because of our honest talks, we were able to incorporate the friendship into our marriage. My son found the original note of our first private meeting and was upset until I explained to him our method of mending our marriage. His comment, "Whatever works, Mom."

6. *You can choose to hold on for a dearer life.*

Your partner has a great need for emotional safety and closeness. There may be times when you will have to put your needs on hold and merely hold her in your arms. One thing that works well for my husband and me is holding one another.

One of my treasured memories occurred after my husband and I were reunited at the airport after a business-related two-month separation. I was greeted at the terminal with his hug of gratitude and heart-felt emotion that extended into being held for a very long time. Airport clamor ceased. Without speaking we rediscovered our love, our togetherness. Holding sessions have been and continue to be a healing balm to our relationship.

Having a partner with a history of sex abuse will give you every opportunity to feel at great odds with your partner, as well as be a compassionate friend, to learn boundaries, and to become more aware of your own needs and capacities.

I look at survivors of abuse as people with an additional purpose whose happiness and peace of mind come at a price. As survivors conquer fear, dare to trust, and even to love, victories pave the way to peace. It takes maturity and a lot of love to be there for a survivor. Those of you who stand by her deserve great appreciation. It is no coincidence your ribbon is blue. You are winners.

CHAPTER 24

Clergy

I added this section at the suggestion of a clergyman who attended a community dinner where an announcement was made concerning this book.

I ask myself, "Who am I to offer input on such an important topic?"

I answer, "I am the voice of the woman on the other side of the desk."

Perhaps by having been there I can help. I have heard various heart breaking incidents of misunderstanding and less than helpful responses given to women who were in need of clergy's counsel and support in the area of sexual abuse issues. The more clergy can understand their own significant role in the healing process, the better for each of us who turn to them for guidance and understanding.

One of my favorite psychiatrists, Dr. Mort Davis, an insightful Jewish doctor, shared with me this viewpoint on the various uses of religion:

> *To psychotic patients religion often becomes a source of delusions, at times, they believe themselves to be Christ, Satan, and so on. To persons suffering with certain character disorders, religion may be used as a challenge to get around the rules, while appearing to be obedient and upstanding; to neurotic individuals, religion is used to further reinforce feelings of shame and unworthiness; to the healthy person, religion is used as a source of growth and of joy.*

The religious views of many women who come to you will have used them to increase their feelings of shame and unworthiness. You will have the blessed opportunity to teach them that religion can be a source of growth, joy and comfort.

During a rough time in my discovery work, I underlined every scriptural reference on joy and happiness. I even drew a heart around the mention of love and the word 'heart.' This project helped me to stay focused on the positive influence my faith could provide.

While attending an incest seminar at the University of Washington, I was impressed to sign up for a class entitled "Spiritual Support for Survivors." The instructor encouraged each of the participants to share the reaction they received from their clergy members in consulting with them on the subject of their abuse. I was shocked by the following remarks:

"I was told to do 20' Hail Marys.' That was it."

"I was told to never tell a soul."

"I was told to repent and beware because I would attract
 further trouble."

In fact, of the fifteen women present, I was the only person who had been treated with respect and support.

The instructor emphasized the tremendous need to teach the clergy how to helpfully respond to women with abuse issues. She had already dedicated her energies to such a task, meeting with councils of various denominations in order to dispel ignorance about CSA and to encourage proper treatment of those seeking assistance from religious leaders.

The day I confessed my suspicion of having been abused, my religious leader received it well. Right off he seemed to believe me, which caused my mouth to drop open because I felt no one would. Part of me was hoping he would not believe me, and then I would not be stuck with such a heavy revelation. On the other hand, if he had indicated that he did not believe me, my basic emotional stability would have been in question.

Just one week before my meeting with this wise leader, I had first wailed to my husband, "I am bad. I cannot go into the church!" The feeling of being a sinner was overpowering, and thus it was natural for me to seek an authority figure for advice. On the following Sabbath, the courage came. I blurted out in desperation, "Can I talk to you right now?" Within the privacy of his office, I told him my fragmented story. With genuine kindness he said, "You'll likely experience a lot of denial from others, especially parents, on this one." I honestly cannot remember the rest of his counsel, as I was still in a state of semi-shock myself. I do know I felt loved, and somehow my shaken self could make it out the door and down the hall to join fellow worshipers.

He had opened his office and his heart to my cry for help. In doing so, he remains one of my male heroes and one who helped me gain trust in the gender. I have sketched a drawing of men who have influenced my life for good entitled, "These I Have Loved." I portrayed him sitting behind his desk and me literally at his mercy. I trust this good man knew by the Spirit my experience was real and that a loving God guided him in his words. It may have also helped that he also had received some training in counseling in this delicate area.

There are women who feel further intimidated if their religious leader sits behind a desk–the desk separates you and implies he has authority over you. Some women resent that this looks like they are now at the mercy of this man. I did not mind that there was furniture between us. You may want to be sensitive to the room arrangement.

Another religious leader, after hearing my history, pounded his fist upon his desk and literally shouted. "How can these things happen to innocent little children?" He was otherwise a man of quiet demeanor. I had the feeling people throughout the building heard him. His anger took me by surprise, but it was very reaffirming to know I was not alone in my anger. But what followed was even better. "You are innocent, Victoria–totally innocent." This good man further advised with full conviction and in a powerful, commanding tone quite unlike his own: "Do not be afraid!"

Reactions of clergymen differ. My experiences were powerful affirmations that these good men, whom I believed were the servants of a loving God, were solidly approving of me. Wow, that felt good! So to you who will be sitting across from those dear women who have been abused, I implore, be prepared!

- **Seek counsel from your church leaders and/or community resources**.

  Study available material and talk with others in your positions who have had experience dealing with CSA victims. Attend Informative classes on abuse issues. The Boy Scout program offers an informative video and class discussion. You may also contact local sexual abuse centers or rape crisis centers for updated and professional classes/information.

At a recent meeting for religious leaders in our immediate community, I was saddened to see the small group that sought additional instruction on issues of abuse. The topic ought to attract the attention of every leader who desires to effectively serve a congregation. I was later informed the organizers of the meeting were hesitant to refer to it as a meeting on abuse, thinking people would avoid attending. This is certainly a commentary on the dilemma of a society that remains confused on how to deal with the topic.

- **If you are the leader of a Christian denomination, look at the woman sitting across from you through Christ-like eyes.** You represent the Lord to the needy, afflicted, and poor in spirit. Having Christ as a role model will give you surprising insights as you respond with His spirit. Being non-judgmental and listening from your heart will cause you to be a blessing in the most critical moments. Offer a safe, sure refuge. See beyond the tear stained face and drooping shoulders.

- **Know your limits.** It is crucial that ignorance and preconceived, biased opinions toward those who have been abused be replaced with updated and supportive beliefs and attitudes conducive to healing. Make it a matter of prayer that you will say and do those things most helpful.

- **Become familiar with local support systems and empathetic therapists**. Do not hesitate to encourage her to seek the method of treatment that will be most effective. In many communities gifted individuals have been trained to assist the abused.

- **Commend her on her progress.** With proper therapy and a strong support system, you will likely witness a transformation, a change in posture and demeanor, with additional sparkle in her eyes.

- **Realize that young women with a history of CSA are more prone to involvement in premarital sexual activity.**
  Many have been programmed by their repressed childhood experiences of exploitation. Their forgotten history could cause them to act out sexually at an early age. Such a history, if available from a resource person who is aware of past abuse, would be important information to obtain as long as it is treated respectfully.

- **Above all, show her respect.**
  You cannot know her anguish. But you can see her as a courageous person daring to confide in you that which she and you wish had never taken place.

CHAPTER 25

Mental Health Technicians

When admitted to the Stress Center of the hospital in a totally collapsed state following a postoperative drug reaction, I was helplessly limp and unable to speak. I believed if I did, I would have another psychotic reaction and would die. I needed to be in a safe place my mind could no longer provide. My history of CSA complicated matters as I reverted to a little child and relived the hellish terror and confusion. I trusted no one, and yet I was in the hands of strangers when my husband and my friend, Pam, left to return home.

Following a neurological exam, catatonia was ruled out, and there I lay. I had given up, yet I was still alive. I dared to move but not to speak and was assigned to a young man, about 25 years old, who stuttered. With my weary mind I thought, "Great, I don't dare speak and he has trouble speaking." He brought me my dinner tray and offered to sit by the side of the bed as I ate. It was a seemingly simple suggestion, and I was immediately grateful. He must have realized how frightened and confused I was. Being alone with my racing, distorted thinking was almost intolerable, and with extremely low blood pressure, I could not be medicated for relief. To this day, when I think of that trial, the picture of that man sitting across from my bedside table remains a comfort. I don't even remember his name and I never thanked him, but he'll remain on my list of personal angels.

While tenderness and compassion are important qualities for all workers assisting in all types of patient care, they are imperative when caring for patients with CSA. Although we are conditioned to think of tenderness and compassion as female qualities, I wish now to pay special tribute to the "gentle men" who have assisted in my care as a patient and with whom I have worked as a mental health nurse.

I have witnessed heart-rending scenes between male staff members and our female patients. One touching example occurred as I rounded the corner leading to the desk area. I observed a young worker reaching across the counter from his seated position to quietly hold the hand of a distraught elderly woman. He was not speaking and neither was she. He just continued holding her hand while looking up at her–and that was just right.

Another fine example of a male mental health worker's sensitivity occurred one evening during my shift. Due to the critical condition of a newly admitted CSA patient who had recently been raped, my fellow worker suggested, "I think it might be easier for her if you do the admitting procedures." I have had the pleasure of working with gentle giants as non-threatening as teddy bears, with men who remain deeply affected as they read patient histories of abuse, with men who quietly go about their work serving the needs of my dear sisters, once abused, with their gifted sense of concern and protectiveness. From a former patient and current nurse's perspective, I appreciate each of you true *gentle* men for your willingness to show respect, mercy, and patience for your female patients, many of whom have rarely known such kindness from men. You are gentlemen in the truest sense.

CHAPTER 26

Physicians/Therapists

I realize that CSA clients/patients, such as I, present challenges to physicians and health care professionals. The following six considerations may be useful to those of you who are key persons in our discovery and recovery processes:

1. ***Combine personal warmth with clinical professionalism in treating clients with CSA.***

When I was in nurse's training, we were taught the rules of being professional, which seemed to offset us from our patients in a way that seemed to give us superiority over them. Only at the end of our training did they teach us it was all right, and even helpful to the patient, to cry with them if we felt impressed to do so. I recognize the importance of setting limits and using professional ethics, yet I appreciate the Bernie Siegel approach depicted in his book, *Love, Medicine and Miracles*, because it removes the desk between patient and professional. Without warmth and caring, a therapist may be lacking the tools that will deeply touch other human beings. I am not a professional counselor, but I respect and admire those of you who have dedicated yourselves to the challenging task. Those in our society who are seeking emotional assistance need you very much. My concern is that you come from your heart, as well as your head, in treating all clients, but particularly those with CSA. Behaviors that encourage trust are those that convey your sincere caring. May I suggest the following:

- Meet your clients at eye level rather than stand above them.

- Refrain from sitting behind a desk when conversing with clients.
- Show primary concern for the patient, rather than their payment method.
- Speak in a soft, clear tone without grimacing responses or flat affects.
- Explain methods of treatment thoroughly and ask for any questions that you may be able to clarify.
- If you are a physician, request permission for touching, even saying before a pelvic exam, "Are you ready?"
- Offer use of medication before traumatic physical treatments and remain non-judgmental.

My own recovery has often been dependent upon therapists, and I shudder to think what might have become of me had I been misdiagnosed or poorly managed. Any amount of disrespect, disbelief, or aloofness during my times of crises would have been devastating to me.

2. *Be astute in gathering initial patient/client information.*

There is debate over whether or not to include the question, "Are you aware of having sexual abuse in your background?" on your initial information-gathering forms, as this is sometimes described as "leading." I was impressed when this question was included in the initial paperwork before my recent yearly gynecological exam with a new doctor. I expressed my appreciation for his questionnaire, which included general and specific abuse questions. He said that he believed these were significant questions to ask.

With a history of CSA (known or unknown), your patients' ability to trust you with their well-being, and even with their lives, may be greatly impaired. The fact that many of you are males can further complicate the scenario. It is immensely helpful if physicians remember that performing invasive and, at times painful, procedures on such patients may trigger old memories and cause distorted reactions that may surprise both of you. This includes oral, rectal, and vaginal intrusions.

When people call in a crisis for nursing advice, I offer referrals to the most caring therapists in town. I also ask them, "Do you have a caring doctor who will listen to you? If so, you can let him or her know what you know about your own history. It can be a strengthening factor in giving you the courage to face any health crisis or health need you might have."

During the discovery phase of my abuse, my primary physician was tremendously supportive. A great example of being right there for me, he made useful suggestions and observations and never caused me to feel additional discomfort or shame.

Several years later, as I was seeking a diagnosis for a gynecological concern over an enlarged ovary initially labeled as a "pelvic mass," the opposite reaction occurred. The initial specialist was sarcastic and eager to schedule me for surgery as soon as possible. In my effort to avoid the trauma of another operation, I consulted with a second doctor. Upon hearing just a few sentences of my abuse history, which I felt was significant to include, the doctor totally changed the subject and looked away. I realized this was someone with whom I could not feel comfortable on this issue, so I contacted another, more nurturing physician.

On my first appointment with the third physician, I briefly explained my background and the extra trauma I was suffering at this time because of a condition that might require surgery. This doctor looked up and gave me his full attention. He remarked, "Gosh, how have you managed to do as well as you are doing today?" He spoke at length with my husband and me, encouraging us to look at each option, and seek guidance from the Spirit. He was a believer in spiritual healing. His physical exam was gentle, yet thorough. At the end of my visit, I felt his respect and caring support, and that was what I had needed in addition to the exam.

3. ***Take the time to get additional education and training in the area of sexual abuse and in techniques that would be helpful to your patients.***

Unfortunately, some doctors are resistant to increasing their understanding of the patient with CSA. I literally chased a hurried psychiatrist down a hospital corridor with the request for him to listen to a tape on the dynamics of sexual abuse that I felt would help a particular patient's treatment and outcome. He questioned, "Victoria, why is it I get the feeling you are trying to convert me?

Why open this can of worms for our patient when she already has enough problems?"

My reply: "Because the worms are already out of the can. They may even be the original source of her symptoms!" Then he listened. I continued using his analogy, "These so-called worms could be fatal to her and she hasn't the energy or ability at this time to get them collected and back into their can as she has done in the past. Shouldn't our hospital unit offer a safe environment where she can deal with and get additional treatment for her worms?" We laughed. He relented, accepted and listened to the tape. The following day, he added to her diagnosis: posttraumatic stress disorder. I shook his hand with gratitude.

Because my mind/body recovery work had such an effect upon my personal recovery process, I am including, with permission, part of my book interview with Robert McDonald, MSW, graduate of the University of California, and international NLP instructor. (see Resources). He offered the following comments:

The entire list of psychologists and counselors whom I know personally are doing the very best they know how to help people who have wounded hearts. They have wonderful intentions and are usually well trained, given the training available. I used to sit down with psychologists who would do reflective listening and I felt so much better that I was understood. While it didn't change my grief or whatever I was dealing with, I thank God they were there and I'm very much in favor of psychologists, therapists and counselors and so on. I also favor them adding to their available techniques those that will tend to get the job done. Abuses happen in every profession. It is important to notice what works and what does not work. I find what works better than anything else is simple kindness. If a person has been abused as a child, I use specific NLP techniques that have been learned through additional training. I have had the opportunity of sharing with clinical workers who treat rape victims, simple and effective methods in treating their intense suffering. Therapists need to take advantage of all the opportunities they can to give them additional tools.

Our mental health unit held an in-service meeting given by Ann, my knowledgeable counselor, on the various ways to improve inpatient care for one of our patients suffering with CSA memories. She encouraged me to share the following transcribed notes that have proven valuable:

Most adults admitted to your unit with abuse issues have lived through a parent's denial and disbelief. They resist disclosure because they have been warned, 'Stop making this up,' or 'You have such an imagination,' which adds to the trauma. This patient was constrained to keep a secret all of her life. She may talk about it in code. Abuse patients often speak in metaphors. Listen carefully for them. An example is, 'A dragon has hold of me.' As far as diagnosis– it is all over the map! All sorts of categories are used for diagnosis of the sexually abused: personality disorders such as borderline, major depression, multiple personality, and manic-depressive. All of these are common for such patients, yet posttraumatic stress disorder is frequently overlooked.

Often victims of sexual abuse understandably demonstrate paranoid behavior. It makes sense because someone they trusted has not been worthy of that trust. This can make any authority figure a threat; even those who are warm and attentive have proven to be damaging. This narrows the path for the caretaker. Nevertheless, be caring; assure a controlled environment and protect her dignity and autonomy. She will likely appear to hate adults and we are adults. Remind her that treatment will release a lot of energy to enable her to get well. (Anger is energy). Help her assimilate the information she is giving herself (through flashbacks or psychotic-like behavior) and assure her it is very meaningful and useful.

When it happened is irrelevant. To the patient, her abuse is very immediate and, until it is dealt with, it can be current. Assuring her it occurred 50 years or so ago is not helpful. Reinforce that it was not her fault, no matter how old she was, and she is a worthwhile person. Remember, sex abuse is like other traumas, but more intense and difficult to recover from. The patient is compelled to review it in her mind, causing unwanted pictures and unwelcome messages to enter her awareness. We all have resistance in realizing people (perpetrators) behave in such ways.

One of the questions asked at the meeting was, "Why do you think our client, who is thirty-five years old, has to continually carry her ragged old doll around with her?" Ann's reply, "It is likely her only witness of what happened to her as a child." It made sense, and making sense of things, even bizarre comments and behaviors of such patients, is one way we can help. Ann had a whole set of tools from which to draw for each particular case.

4. *Come from the inner place of wisdom (some refer to it as being guided by the Spirit) when making decisions and responding to persons with histories of sexual abuse.*

As a worker in this critical area, one needs to be in tune to that voice which goes beyond the training received in formal education. Intuition also comes from experience. The following true account is my most effective example of our need to have a sense for the additional considerations required for those patients who have CSA:

Julia's Spells

Julia was in a state of excruciating trauma, mumbling and swearing. Her body and expressions were distorted by fear. It was simple to suppose her behavior was the evidence of psychoses; clearly, she was not in reality.

The information on our new admission was sketchy, with recent deep depression as the more distressing and debilitating symptom. Her husband had been desperately seeking relief measures for his troubled wife who, in his own words, "had flipped out." Deanne and I were working together as staff nurses on the small eight-bed hospital mental health unit. We worked quickly to get Julia into a private room and reviewed the doctor's orders. Julia was so unsettled and out of control, I resorted to drawing up an injection we commonly used for psychotic patients.

I shall never forget how the two of us entered her room, studied her for a moment and looked searchingly at one another. Both of us were impressed simultaneously not to give the prepared injection. This was not a typical psychosis. It was not a book or training-learned understanding that impressed us, but the inner sense (which is always welcomed) that spoke to us. My partner left the room to attend to other patients. I asked John, the patient's husband, to speak clearly to his wife and reassure her she was safe and he was there to help her. After a few moments, she let him massage her back.

His reassurance continued. I slipped out into the waiting room where her exhausted-looking elderly mother sat resolutely. It was a long shot, but worth a try. I knelt down in order to be eye level with her. "Nadine," I began, "is it possible your daughter was ever sexually abused as a child?" She squirmed in the chair and in an irritated tone, she replied, "Well, yes." "By someone close to her?" I asked. "Never could trust my old man," she answered. "She was his favorite, you know, always spent his money on her, not me. He even bothered a little girl on the bus and had me lie for him."

I returned to Julia's room and asked her husband to join me in the hall for a moment. "John, are you aware of the possibility your wife was molested as a child? I believe she may be reliving the experience in a flashback of her past. She is neither crazy nor psychotic," I finished. With his permission, I simply told Julia she was likely reliving an incident from her past. I assured her we were there to help her and she was not crazy. She responded with relaxed muscles. He rubbed her back, speaking quietly for 10 minutes. I then repeated my information. She sat up on the side of the bed and remarked with relief, "That makes sense." She later joined the other patients in the eating area and ate her dinner while conversing with them. Her husband thanked us. "This is really a breakthrough and very helpful. Now it is making sense. Thank you. This is the best my wife has been after one of her "spells." Although she continued to be treated for depression, posttraumatic stress disorder (PTSD) became her modified diagnosis.

What are clues that persons with PTSD are not hallucinating? It is often difficult to differentiate because, in fact, a major flashback is seeing and hearing things others cannot perceive. As with a typical psychosis those suffering with PTSD do compulsive things that do not make sense to you, but are meaningful to that individual. I have seen little old ladies wander around muttering 'no,' and 'I am bad, so bad.' They are overly apologetic, at times may be hypersexual, may disrobe, or may be found in a child-like state curled up in a corner of their room. We need to consider that such bizarre behavior may stem from a flashback condition.

In one instance, at the suggestion of a wise neurologist, I was able to console a patient in this confused, regressed condition. I told her I believed she was having a flashback. I added that I understood them and had experienced them myself. She threw her arms around me, immediately losing her glassy stare and rigid posture, and spoke in her adult voice instead of little whimpers. We have much to learn.

5. *Become aware of those persons and programs in your community best qualified to treat your clients/patients with issues of CSA should you decide to suggest a referral.*

Insight and experience in the field are useful. That is one reason my physician advised me to call Ann, who was known for her work with abuse victims, about my initial flashback. She was the first person I dared to tell over the phone of my secret. Her calm, reassuring voice will always be with me. She told me I could call her day or night. Only once did I call after a confusing flashback at 2 a.m. I'll never forget her reply: "Yes, Victoria, what is it, dear, that's troubling you? I am so pleased you called. Maybe I can help." Whenever I am tempted to yell at myself, Ann's voice is there, loving me unconditionally. I appreciate doctors and therapists who are willing to have people contact them as needed. Yet in order to refrain from overusing that right, my occasional late-night calls are best met by phone calls to the crises 800 lines. Sharing with a trained listener (and a total stranger 'out there' somewhere) has been comforting. Therapists often include a crises number with their answering message.

6. *Help your patient/client reduce incidents of vicarious traumatization*

Unfortunately, even talking about past trauma can bring forward unwanted trauma discomfort for those of us with abuse histories. In some instances, as with my own experience, clients may seek information for which they are not prepared.

Hypnosis

At one point in my therapy, I requested the use of hypnosis in order to find out additional information about my history. (Perhaps a morbid curiosity led me to dig further into my past.) I had previously found hypnosis to be very useful in working with visualizations, and positive affirmations.

Even though I had absolute trust in the highly trained therapist, I began to get nauseated on the drive to her office. I felt that something was definitely *coming up.* (Over time, I learned to more quickly recognize what was happening.) As she guided me into a trance, I remember my last conscious thought was, "I'm not going to tell." At the conclusion of the session, she returned me to my former state of amnesia. It was her belief that my subconscious mind's need to suppress some information should be respected. I agreed, and to this day, I remember no details of the session. Even with her additional amnesia precaution, I was severely retraumatized and remained physically ill for twenty-four hours. It is important to realize that the nausea and anxiety was in place prior to the hypnosis session and that even without it I may have suffered from the memory that was surfacing. I learned that it is best to allow my mind to reveal information to me at it's own pace. I do not plan to pursue any further uncovering of my childhood memories. If they surface, they surface. If they don't, then more information may not be relevant to my recovery. I continue to enjoy self-hypnosis techniques for relaxation, and I appreciate the resulting trance-like state.

I am in agreement with this information given specifically to therapists in Adena Bank Lee's lecture on Sexual Abuse issues:

Hypnosis should not be used for memory retrieval. Memory retrieval must be approached carefully. Therapists should assess in an on-going manner clients' abilities to handle the potential content of new memories. Patience, as opposed to pressure, with the remembering process is important for both the therapist and the client.

Because expressive techniques often recreate the affective state of the original trauma, they should be used with caution because they have the potential to retraumatize the client. Although expressive techniques have the potential to facilitate clients' working through and integrating of the trauma, clients must be able to handle the level of emotional intensity [1-5]

Group Therapy

It is my opinion that group participants should have an on-going supportive therapist during the period of time in which they are attending such sessions. I also appreciate this additional insight from Adena's workshop:

Group treatment can be very effective for CSA issues, especially in reducing shame and isolation. Client's in group treatment for CSA should have clear memories (or at least memory of one incident of CSA), not just suspect they may have been sexually abused. If the group treatment includes clients' sharing of abuse incidents, group members must be strong enough to hear others' stories without being retraumatized (vicarious traumatization). To prevent second wounding, group norms of believing and not blaming need to be established. [1-5]

7. *Be positive and supportive, an advocate for the CSA patient.*

Another physician, a hero deserving of mention, was my psychiatrist at a neighboring hospital's mental health unit established for patients in need of 24-hour emotional support. When I had my so called 'breakdown,' the gentle, bearded doctor attentively listened to my husband's account of my collapsed state and responded with reassurance that I was suffering from a reaction from the drug, Prednisone which would require four days to clear my system. My racing, manic-like thinking would then be resolved. They would medicate me carefully, and the much-needed sleep would decrease the likelihood of a second psychotic episode. I later learned while I was being taken to my assigned room, he continued, "Victoria's symptoms (hysteria and an unwillingness to talk) are consistent with her history of sexual abuse." I remember his daily visit to my bedside. One day he held my hand and said, "Victoria, you made it through incest, and you'll make it through this." This man was aware of the dynamics of sexual abuse, and he used my background to strengthen me. On day three I could think clearly enough to write to him. I expressed gratitude and my determination to fully recover.

Upon my discharge 10 days later, we met in the designated quiet room, with its soft lights and colorful fish aquarium. He sat directly across from me in a similar comfortable chair–no desk, no papers. He reassured me that with time I would become desensitized. He advised me to use a tranquilizer as needed and to study the suggested books on anxiety. I had a difficult road ahead, but he set me out on the right path.

An additional wise therapist greatly assisted in my healing process. Dr. Ron Minson offered the firm, yet gentle caring that increased my trust in him and toward men in general, as he treated my post-op depression and PTSD. He adamantly and successfully defended my position as a survivor of sexual abuse when he faced my insurance company representatives. He was indignant over their unfair assumption that with my background I would need extensive therapy for the rest of my life. They contended that a condensed program would not affect my long-term needs. As a survivor myself, I know psychotherapy need not always be long and drawn out. It depends on the individual, the extent of her abuse, and her symptoms. Some self-help methods are proving to be effective complements to therapy.

Change is challenging and frightening. Establishing healthier beliefs and reactions requires awareness and practice. As survivors, many of us seem to have periods of reduced or absent symptoms, with occasional bouts of symptoms that demand attention, even the assistance of a therapist. Then, with treatment, we are able to move forward once again, a little wiser and stronger and with additional understanding.

True or False Memories?

Having some symptoms typical of sexual abuse is not proof positive a person was abused sexually. This area needs to be explored carefully, and guidelines are available in the books *Memory and Abuse* by Charles Whitfield and *Memory, Trauma, Treatment and the Law* by Daniel Brown.

There seems to be a great deal of interest in the question of where the truth lies when a female believes she has a CSA background. It would be convenient if we had a list of symptoms with the conclusion that by checking off 15 out of 20, the history of CSA would be verified. Such is not the case. Unfortunately for many, the CSA diagnosis remains a judgment call, and the demanding dilemma of 'was she or wasn't she' sexually abused continues. Scientific studies are underway that may one day be useful in this area.

I can speak only for myself and from my own circumstance in knowing for sure I was molested as a child. I cannot tell others whether their experience really happened, or whether their daughter's or their friend's claims of sexual abuse are actual or not. I understand the issues and that families can be destroyed by unfair attack from both positions. The most prayerful consideration needs to be given in such cases. As in cases of medical conditions, I also recommend a second or third opinion from additional therapists whose views may be helpful.

Following an explicit, sexually related anxiety attack years before my major flashback, my therapist questioned if I had any childhood trauma. I flatly refused to even consider the possibility. The therapist pointed out reasons for her suspicion, which seemed mildly valid. Did the therapist plant the notion of my abuse? No, she recognized some of the symptoms. She was right on–but I was not ready to receive the truth. She respected me enough to go on with treatment of the symptoms of depression with unusual anxiety reactions. My first major flashback in the church parking lot was certainly not a memory recovery technique! Today's qualified therapists have guidelines to follow that are supportive and not suggestive.

I believe our own subconscious mind will know when the abuse memories should be made manifest if, indeed, they are part of our past. My abuse made sense of my symptomatic history. Untreated symptoms of abuse have been indelibly etched upon my life and the lives of too many others plagued with undue guilt, anguish and distress. I have advised those who recognize such symptoms to do as I did and seek resolution and treatment and to trust if they do have what they suspect are indications of CSA. It will be revealed personally at the necessary time. Proper and timely therapy will likely be beneficial either way. If individuals express to me that they feel they are being "pushed" by their therapist to explore the CSA issue when they have no awareness of such history, I advise them to change to another counselor. I am so grateful my abuse revelation came at a time when knowledge and understanding had been sufficiently gleaned by those who believed me and that proper direction and treatment were given.

It is important to remain honest and aware concerning childrens' abuse. Early recognition and treatment before time elapses will prevent it from becoming a memory issue.

True or false memories of childhood sexual abuse? That will remain a question for some people, but not for those of us who have been given the answer, whether we like it or not.

Notes

1. APA Division 17 Task Force on Memories of Childhood Sexual Abuse (1995). Recommendations for working with clients who may have an abuse or trauma history. Self-published document.

2. Enns, C.Z., Campbell, J., Courtois, C.A., Gottlieb, M.C., Lese, K.P., Gilbert, M.S., & Forrest, L, (In press). Working with adult clients who may have experienced childhood abuse: Recommendations for assessment and practice. *Professional Psychology*.

3. Enns, C.Z., McNeilly, C.L., & Gilbert, M.S. (1995). The debate about delayed memories of child sexual abuse: A feminist perspective. The *Counseling Psychologist*, 23, 181-270.

4. Pam Remer, Ph.D., Presentation at ASGPP Annual Meeting, April, 1998.

5. Adena Bank Lees, CISW, ICADC. Presentation for certified class on Sexual Abuse. Helping Adult & Child Survivors, 1998.

CHAPTER 27

Advantages of Using Spiritual Beliefs

The stresses of living in today's complex world have prompted many people to look for relief through a higher power, providing them with reassurance, warmth and love that exceed common experience. Spirituality helps people to move into a more peaceful, fulfilling realm, to function on a higher level. The practice of meditation, in whatever form, gives persons a 'safe place,' an internal refuge. Most people now realize that prayer is a powerful form of meditation, and that they can increase their experience by entering into it with calm deliberation. People knowledgeable about alternative methods are becoming more in touch with themselves, and are seeking to be influenced by a higher power.

When spiritual needs are determined and respected, a patient's chance of recovery from emotional, as well as physical disorders is greatly enhanced. I will share the following three examples of spiritual interventions that were useful for me:

Painted Angels

One afternoon during my treatment at the Center for Innerchange, I felt tremendous anxiety when some powerful emotions surfaced. A perceptive assistant listened as I related that I felt I could not continue in the Tomatis program outlined for me on the following day. She drew to my attention that I seemed to be painting robed figures in some of my drawings and then asked me, "Do you believe in angels?"

"Yes," I replied.

"Then for tomorrow's therapy session, you might want to pray for angels to be with you for protection and comfort, because some pretty tough stuff is coming up into your awareness."

I did as she suggested and received strength for the following day's task. As a result, my belief in angels and the comfort they can give increased.

At Least You Have Your Faith

How often I had taken for granted the blessing of being able to read the scriptures from my favorite large-print copy. Following my brain operation, I requested having the beloved book brought to me simply to hold. Since I had acquired sterile meningitis with a resulting cortisone reaction, I could not read. My brain was in an organic state–my memory was shot. I would shower and forget where I had already washed. I did not know where I was and though I recognized people, I requested no visitors. I could barely speak because it confused me. In fact, the first two days I did not talk at all. The doctor said it would take four days for the Prednisone effects to wear off. A nurse kindly reminded me, "You are going to make it. At least you have your faith!" At first, I felt the burden of her expectation. I was frightened beyond expression. Even my prayers seemed disjointed and confusing because I could not think clearly and my head throbbed. I appreciated her reminder of my faith as an available resource. On the second night, another patient of the unit entered my room and asked if she could pray with me. I consented and meekly welcomed her into my quarters. She was of another faith and was eager to share her sweet and lengthy scripture-filled prayer. I marveled that she had such a memory and was envious, but very grateful for her attention to my starving soul. She emphasized a biblical scripture from 2nd Timothy 1:7, which reads: "For God hath not given us the spirit of fear; but of power, and of love, and of a sound mind."

Never had a scripture held more hope for me than this one in my desperate hour. I asked her to please write it on a slip of paper. She handed it to me, and we hugged. With my partially-shaven head and deliberate wide steps for balance, I walked the halls clinging to the piece of paper with the few words on it that I could read and comprehend. Still unable to memorize, I just read it over and over again as I believed and waited for my sound mind to return.

On day three, unable to speak well, I painstakingly wrote a letter to the doctor telling him I would recover. I listed the reasons–my family, my religion, my Lord, my friends, and lots of prayers. He agreed. On day four, my system was free of infection and medication. I could think clearly, write readily, and I could read and comprehend. It was as if I had been an eighty-year-old with dementia, and then released back into being forty-three. I memorized my favorite scripture and referred to it frequently as I continued the road to recovery.

During the above-mentioned hospitalization, I had tremendous difficulty falling asleep. With very low blood pressure, receiving a sedative was risky, so the nursing staff was doing their best to help me sleep. A relaxation tape had helped the previous night but it was missing, so a sweet night nurse sat by my bed and quietly fed me pleasant affirmations, soothing thoughts, including the message, "God loves you." She repeated the live messages until I drifted off into welcomed sleep. I believe in living angels. She qualified.

VII

TRANSITION FROM VICTIM TO THRIVER

Life, at best, is a journey, with alternating stops and starts, arrivals, resting times, anticipation of new destinations to be reached. . . . for the victim of CSA, life is a journey toward recovery, marked by at least three distinct and progressively healthy attitudes towards the abuse suffered.

Irene Perrins

CHAPTER 28

Victim

Where is Your Past?

With a history of CSA, we all had our beginning in the position of 'victim.' However, maintaining a victim position is a guaranteed method of maintaining misery. Clinging to memories of mistreatment leaves one hanging in an unkind world. Assuming that all of my problems and weaknesses as an adult have been the result of CSA is assuming my victim mentality. Many of you probably remember the 'Twilight Zone', a television series depicting the miserable state of those who found themselves in such a confusing place. Similar, and at times equally bizarre, is the 'Victim Zone,' complete with loneliness, distortions, confusion and powerlessness.

I witnessed an amazing reaction in a classroom situation where the instructor, Robert McDonald, respectfully asked a class member, "Where is your past if you were to point to it in this room?" The man pointed directly in front of him. The instructor then carefully lifted the imaginary past and put it behind the man, who immediately sat up straighter in his chair. "I feel better than I have in years," the man exclaimed with amazement. "I feel so much lighter." Robert's next comment was interesting, "Those with abusive backgrounds may find their past is in front of them, and as a result, they keep repeating old patterns, rather than having a fresh new perspective." One person in the class could not bear to have his past moved from the front of him. Class members who could tolerate the adjustment felt emptiness at first, then a feeling of openness and a future with more possibilities.

Robert taught that people with abuse in their backgrounds are often walking through their past, rather than putting it aside or behind them. As long as the past is in front, the individual has the same perspective and outlook as in the past. This perspective makes one feel trapped. It also allows abuse to continue. There are skillful, and often subtle, ways to rearrange the past.

The greatest discovery of my generation is that human beings can alter their lives by altering their attitude of mind.
William James

Victim Zone

When enmeshed in the unhealthy parts of my childhood, emotional pain engulfs me. My inward cries are, "Poor me," "Life is not fair," "Why me?" or "I am trapped." I feel small and powerless. I want to be rescued. I will use my husband's weaknesses to reinforce my feelings that life is awful. I become very critical. Money concerns become overwhelming. At those times, I have entered into the Victim Zone. Non-victim outsiders, who recognize where I am, enter either briefly or not at all. When other victims combine their zone with mine, there is little comfort.

Although outsiders can recognize my position, there are times I do not realize when I am in the Victim Zone. Awareness has shown me the responses of those close to me give obvious clues. They do not want to be around me. This reinforces my original position, in which I am alone and unwanted and I feel full of resentment. That seems to go with the Victim Zone territory. One of the frustrations in watching the 'Twilight Zone' series was it would simply end without resolution, leaving the viewers in a weird state of wondering. The good news concerning the Victim Zone is that there is a way (or several ways) out. The following exercises have helped me to be free from the its influence:

Victim Zone Escape Routes

- **Switch instantly to a better frame of mind**
  Using an NLP strategy, I imagine the Victim Zone existing around me as no larger than a five-foot diameter circle and then I choose to step out into a kinder, more rational world. What a relief!

- **Kneel in prayer and offer thanks.**
  That means I must find something for which to be grateful. This challenges my victim position. This process can take a while when I remain stubbornly stuck in self-pity. Then comes a softening, and finally relief.

- **Request help from above**
  I am a great believer in angels. Requesting their presence has also been useful.

- **Ask a trusted friend to help you**
  An objective, kind friend can identify when you act and/or look as if you are in the Victim Zone. Tone of voice, posture and general hopelessness are big clues.

- **Lighten up**
  Be creative. Laugh tenderly at your tendency to travel in such crummy places of mind and spirit, and never give up in the quest to move into a brighter existence.

- **Follow experts' advice**
  Take the time to read some good books to strengthen your resolve to exit the financial victim zone. An excellent resource is: *Your Money or Your Life* by Joe Dominguez and Vicki Robin.

CHAPTER 29

Survivor

Not All of Us Survive

While attending a conference organized specifically for women with incest backgrounds, I was impressed with the opening address given by the keynote speaker. She graciously welcomed each of us, thanked those who had traveled great distances, and offered the hope that by the next year's conference, many more would be able to attend. Her next comment sent a chill up my spine: "I also wish to recognize those who will never be able to join us because they are no longer alive."

Having worked with many suicidal patients who barely survived their attempt to end their lives, I often have reminders that not all do survive. Staying alive can require great determination. Every survivor of sexual abuse is first a victim of sexual abuse. But not every victim of sexual abuse is a survivor.

There are three critical areas to keep in mind:

1. Surviving beyond the original childhood abuse is a task often taken on by our subconscious mind.

2. Surviving flashbacks is a challenge because the desire to die is very powerful for many victims. For me, the initial flashback could have been fatal because my judgment was so poor. For example, I could have taken too many pain pills without caring about the consequences.

3. The ensuing depression and physical illnesses take a huge toll. I suspect there are more casualties than we realize. It is likely

increased risks for diseases such as cancer, chronic fatigue syndrome and fibromyalgia plague the unrecognized (and recognized) formerly abused among us. One casual friend of mine confessed to me following her life-threatening bout with colon cancer, "I never told a soul until today that I was molested as a child." I could not help but wonder if there was a connection between her cancer and the untold abuse. Perhaps the stress of keeping secrets knotted up inside affects our auto-immune system, opening us up to a multitude of illnesses and diseases.

Stuck in the Survival Mode

When you get into a tight place, and everything goes against you til it seems as if you couldn't hold on a minute longer, never give up then, for that's the time and place that the tide will turn.

Harriet Beecher Stowe

Just as some victims seem to spend their time in the Victim Zone, others can become stuck in the survival mind set. Staying in the survival mode gives us a feeling of "just barely getting by," and "working hard without getting anywhere." It is a feeling of scarcity and inadequacy, in spite of our efforts to feel capable and abundant. Although familiar, it feels frightening to stay there. It takes a true attitude change to exit this way of thinking.

We have many documented examples of individuals with AIDS, Cancer and numerous other illnesses, who have recovered when their attitude about the illness allowed them to think about it in a positive way. We can use this understanding to increase our own chances of healing and recovery.

I congratulate each of us for having survived. Can we now look on being a CSA survivor as an opportunity to overcome, to learn from, to give us additional self-love and faith? Yes, I believe so. If you can similarly believe, you are headed for the great adventure of 'thriving.' It is time to move on.

CHAPTER 30

Thriver

It is widely known among professionals in the field (and within a growing general population), that a background of abuse can produce pathology ranging from somatic illness, phobias, eating disorders, and suicidal ideation to full psychotic-like behavior. I would like to identify some *positive* results, however. You may question whether there can be positive results. Yes, numerous individuals have emerged as survivors, with a growing number of them becoming what I like to refer to as 'thrivers.' Through acknowledgment, carefully selected treatment, and allowing the healing process to occur, the thrivers live rich lives, full of hope and love. These unsung heroes are in our midst everywhere.

I have been exposed to the idea of thriving when in counseling with Dr. Ron Minson during my recovery and while researching for this book. As a psychiatrist, he firmly believes women with abuse histories can fully recover and live joyful lives free of victimization. He labeled me as a thriver. Although I questioned his judgment at the time, I determined to live up to the title. It certainly sounded better than the labels of "depressed and sufferer of posttraumatic stress disorder" necessary for diagnosis and insurance purposes. I came up with my own definition of thriver, since it was not in my dictionary as such. A thriver, within the context of sexual abuse, is one who:

- Has abuse in her past, healing in her present, and hope in her future
- Prospers emotionally from developing her resources
- Has a sense of personal abundance that stems from within and is evidenced in all that she does
- Is able to grow vigorously toward reaching her divine destiny

- Uses her capacity for joyful living in loving, sensitive ways
- Recognizes the source of her light

This is merely my picture of a thriver. You can certainly add to it with your own use of desired powerful words and impressions. Imagine the action flowing from the following words associated with thrivers:

Living	Discovering	Blossoming
Growing	Becoming	Creating
Extending	Loving	Participating
Reaching	Exploring	Regenerating
Partaking	Being	Rejoicing

In the eyes of a thriver, the fullness of life has been threatened, not destroyed.

My thriver mentality is far from perfect or consistent. When I incorporate it into my daily living, it feels so much better than merely surviving. It is like the differences between drowning (victim), treading water (survivor), and swimming gracefully with strength (thriver).

The Gift

While attending a national conference for survivors, I overheard a young woman lament, "Finding out I was abused and now having to live with it is just awful." A woman standing beside her said reassuringly, "You will find a way. Look at the opportunity this provides you for growth."

"But I don't want it," she replied.

"It is still your gift."

A gift? I pondered over her unusual comment. How, on earth, could anything so awful as being sexually molested as a child be considered a gift? Rather, it seems it should be life's most miserable curse. I shared the young woman's apprehension over the term.

It was from Mia, a therapist with a history of abuse, that this concept of the gift developed from our discussion about her own personal healing. Mia explained, "In the beginning, it would have been really hard for me to hear that an abuse background is a gift, but it is. In the beginning I could only think, 'This is gross.' Somebody did this to me and I hate this man–and there is no way this is a gift. This is the most horrible thing that happened to me on earth and it ruined my life. I would have hated someone telling me then that it is a gift. And now, two years later, I really feel like it is." As she spoke in a gentle tone, her countenance radiating warmth, I treasured each word coming from one who has drawn from a potentially disastrous history a reservoir of love and truth. I have saved the tape of her interview so I can recapture that time together as we shared spirit to spirit our values, lessons learned, and even laughter. We rejoiced together in the excitement of eating the elephant one bite at a time.

In reflecting on the times in my life when I truly have needed comfort, I realized many of my personal angels who stood by me under any circumstances, were adults with a background of abuse. Along with my desire to write this book has come the opportunity to meet with women who possess a tremendous depth of caring and sensitivity, women who have experienced the worst type of trauma. Tragedy can direct lives for good.

Additional examples of unwanted gifts came forward at one of our local community offerings for people suffering with fibromyalgia. When I asked the unusually small gathering of local sufferers what gifts had come from their condition, they were clueless. Then the responses began. "I've come to know myself better." "I've learned to pace myself." "I no longer work at the job I disliked." "I've grown closer to my family." "I have started an exercise program." The list of gifts covered the blackboard.

Having served as a volunteer nurse in NYC following the 911 disasters, I realized how unspeakable tragedy and trauma gave me gifts of increased compassion, endurance, spiritual strength, resolve to strengthen relationships, and willingness to take risks.

Purpose with a Powerful Past

I had a dear friend, not yet aware of my background, once comment to me. "I think people who have had incest in their backgrounds are automatically worthy of heaven." What a sweet thought. While I cannot imagine having an automatic ticket to heaven, let's think for a moment what possible advantages we may have. I am speaking for all of us who have been seriously mistreated in our tender childhood. We do share a common factor, that of a powerful past. We can refer to our pasts as "devastating," "destructive," and "abusive," or we can refer to our POWERFUL past. Power represents energy. We have the challenge of changing the energy of a negative painful past, which can be destructive, into a positive and healthy present and future. Suffering has its necessary place in the lives of all, yet some of it can be relieved in order to free us for a more joyful journey through this life. Used positively, the power from our past contributes to a thriver mentality. Our change from a life of pain to a life of health, forgiveness, and self-empowerment gives others a role model to follow. With the nature of our backgrounds, we can speak with authority about survival techniques.

Once, after a particularly meaningful therapy session, a counselor declared, "Victoria, let the world know you are a force to be dealt with." I felt strength in her words with increased capacity for action. Although math was my weakest subject in college, I envisioned V^5, or Victoria to the Fifth Power! Positive power is divine in nature. When we consider having a continual source of power greater than ourselves, it is like we have the advantage of power steering throughout our lives.

"Old Red"

"Old Red" was our faithful Ford pickup truck. Of all our vehicles on the farm, Old Red was the most dependable. However, Old Red did not have power steering. I remember well the struggle of attempting to turn that old truck quickly in order to avoid becoming stuck in the mud. I'd be pulling with all of my might, even asking one of the boys to pull with me as I'd rev the motor, groan and laugh. With all due respect to Old Red, power steering has great advantages. Our refusal to use higher power can compare to going through this life without power steering.

Once we determine to use our past for the good of others, opportunities will open up that may be surprising. During my stay in Denver, I was made aware that my own experience might be helpful to others. I visited the Kemp Children's Center with a desire to gain more insight into their program for assisting children and families of abuse. Although such programs as this were non-existent in 1949, I imagined what it would have been like for me as a child to enter this building. Even in my forties, it was immensely gratifying to be treated with such validation and acceptance. It is never too late to appreciate finding a safe place. I briefly told the staff of my desire to write a book on child abuse because of my own history. I felt honored, not shamed. They gave me access to files filled with articles and research. The director invited me to join him in his office, where he asked that I teach him and others of my journey of discovery and recovery. As I walked out of the Kemp Center, I felt satisfied dedicated people are working to help children suffering with abuse problems, and I gained strength in my own resolution to join in this effort.

I used to believe that because of my history of abuse, I somehow became weaker, damaged for life, and recovery would never be possible. I used to believe I was permanently different and doomed to a greater amount of sorrow than the more fortunate ones without such a history.

I used to believe . . . .

It is good to have an end to journey towards; but it is the journey that matters in the end.

Ursula K. LeGuin

The Healing Process Timetable

My readers suggested that I include a chronology to be used as reference of events and their influence in my recovery.

Date	Age	Happening	Results
1945		Victoria's birth	Beginning of earth experience
1948	3	Auto accident comfort	Survival, parental support
		Sexual abuse by Grandpa in Laramie, Wyoming	Survival, locked-in secrets, insecurity, nightmares, confusion, loss of trust
		Tonsil party	Survival
1949	4	Parents divorce, move to another state	Abandonment
1952	7	Mother's remarriage	Resentment
1958	13	Puberty Return to school	School phobia, compulsive behavior, eating disorder, somatic ills, depression, psycho-therapy
1960	16	Schooling/college	Intellectualism, achievement, excelling.
1964	21	Marriage/motherhood	Great satisfaction mothering
1980	35	Post-Partum Depression Touching preschool program	Therapy
1987	42	Return of hidden memory	Terror, pain, nightmares, therapy, return of fun-loving, fuller life, authentic self emerged, faith, trust
1988	43	Confronted by Grandma Major surgery	Shut down, physical MS-like illness Survival, regression to terror, collapse, 2-week psychological hospitalization with diagnosis of PTSD
1989	44	Relocation	Hidden depression, chronic fatigue, six months psycho-therapy, emotional upheaval
1990	45	Impression to write book	More healing
1992	47	Tomatis Center	Return to joyfulness, music, art, singing
1994	49	Fibromyalgia Facing disability	*Secret Garden* revived desire to heal further. Medication trials, physical therapy, additional alternative therapies, nutrition, massage
1996	50	Retraining	Increased strength
1997	51	Return to work force	Opportunities to help others increased
1999	53	TLP Training	Ability to share Tomatis experience
2003	57	Completion of Book	Relief

RESOURCES

NLP

"Neuro" refers to the mind and how we organize our mental life. "Linguistic" refers to our use of language and its how it affects us. "Programming" (or "Processing") means our sequence of repetitive behavior and how we act with purpose.

For additional information and free literature contact:
Anchor Point Associates, Inc.
Phone: 801-534-1022

Survivors of Incest Anonymous, Inc.

www.siawso.org
P.O. Box 190
Benson, MD, 21018
Phone: 410-983-3322
Will provide material and support plus group locations

Voices in Action Inc. (Victims of Incest Can Emerge Survivors)

www.voices-action.org
P.O. Box 13
Newton Ville, OH, 45103
1-800-7-VOICE-8
non-profit clearinghouse to assist the adult survivor of CSA

The Center for InnerChange

www.centerforinnerchange.com
4610 So. Ulster St.
Suite 170
Denver, Colorado 80237
303-3204411

This center, directed by Ron Minson, M.D., provides a unique blend of innovative (treatment) modalities combining traditional psychotherapy with music, art, and light therapy plus advanced NLP techniques. By recommending this center, I have witnessed the healing results in lives of many individuals who have made the trip to the center in Denver.

Dynamic Listening System, Inc.
www.dynamiclistening.com
Phone: 1-877-320-5502

In order to further promote the work of Dr. Alfred Tomatis, Dr. Ron Minson has developed a training program in auditory education for educators, musicians, counselors and health care professionals.

The Tomatis Method
www.tomatis.com

Dr. Alfred Tomatis spent his life discovering sound techniques that have a therapeutic effect. He uncovered the importance of high frequency sounds to promote attentiveness, alertness and creativity. His later research led further into the treatment of medical, psychological, educational and attention problems such as Meniere's Disease, dyslexia, depression and anxiety, and Attention Deficit Disorder. His work (that continues today in over 200 Tomatis Centers throughout the world), demonstrates how listening abilities also influence communication thereby shaping social development, confidence and self-image.

TLP The Listening Program® , TLP
Advanced Brain Technologies, LLC
www.advancedbrain.com
P.O. Box 1088
Ogden, Utah, 84402
Email: infor@advancedbrain.com
Ph. 801.6625676
Fax. 801.6274505

This sound-stimulation auditory retraining method consists of eight specially developed CDs with a Guidebook and Listening Journal. The eight-week program can be used at home, school, or office–a CD player and headphones are the only equipment necessary. It is available exclusively through therapists and health and educational professionals who have received specialized training in the administration of the program. TLP is an invitation to active listening, which enhances the function of the ear and brain naturally. As natural listening increases, so do language, attention, and communication skills. As a participant and a provider, I highly recommend this excellent program that builds upon many of the original concepts of Alfred Tomatis, M.D. To order direct from my office contact: victorialynn@aradiance.com

The Sound Health ® Series
Advanced Brain Technologies, LLC
www.advancedbrain.com
P.O. Box 1088
Ogden, Utah, 84402
Email: info@advancedbrain.com
Ph. 801.6625676
Fax. 801.6274505

The Sound Health Series improves the function of the ear and brain by creating a sound capsule of natural full-spectrum sound. It uses psychoacoustically refined orchestrations of Mozart, Bach, Vivaldi, and others, performed by The Arcangelos Chamber Ensemble. These soothing as well as stimulating recordings from the Sound Health Series should be played throughout the day at a very gentle volume to improve auditory processing, to diminish the negative effects of noise pollution, and to enhance health, learning and productivity. Music samples can be heard by using TLP website.

BIBLIOGRAPHY
and SUGGESTED READING

Burnett, Frances Hodgson, *The Secret Garden,*
    HarperCollins, New York, NY, 1962

Brown, Daniel, Alan W. Scheflin and D. Corydon Hammond,
    Memory*, Trauma Treatment, and the Law.*
    W. W. Norton & Company, New York, London, 1998

Bourne, Edmund J., Ph.D., *The Anxiety and Phobia Workbook,*
    New Harbinger Publications, Inc., New York, 1990

Campbell, Don, *Music and Miracles*,
    Wheaton, Ill, Quest Books, 1992

DeAngeleis, Barbara, *Real Moments for Lovers,*
    Dell Publishing, New York, 1995

Dominguez, Joe and Vicki Robin, *Your Money Or Your Life,*
    Penguin Books, New York, NY, 1992

Elgin, Suzette Haden, Ph.D., *You Can't Say That to Me,*
    John Wiley & Sons, Inc. New York, 1995

Farmer, Steven, *Adult Children of Abusive Parents,*
    Ballantine Books, New York, 1990

Gil, Eliana, Ph.D., *Outgrowing the Pain,*
    Dell Publishing, NY, 1983

Hemfelt, Robert, Minirth, and Meier, *Love is a Choice*
    Thomas Nelson Publishers, Nashville, Tennessee, 1989

Hon Kabat-Zinn, Ph.D., *Full Catastrophe Living,*
    Dell Publishing, New York, 1990

Johnson, Barbara, *So, Stick a Geranium in Your Hat and Be Happy,*
    W. Publishing Group, USA, 1990

Latham, Glenn L., *The Power of Positive Parenting,*
   P&T Ink, Inc., Logan, Utah, 1994

Leeds, Joshua, *The Power of Sound,*
   Healing Arts Press, Vermont, 2001

Patricia Love with Jo Robinson, *Emotional Incest*
   Bantam Book, New York, 1990

Maduale, Paul,, *When Listening Comes Alive.*
   Moulin Publishing, Norval, Ontario, 1993.

Miller, Alice, *The Drama of the Gifted Child,*
   Basic Books, USA 1981

Muller, Wayne, *Legacy of the Heart,*
   Fireside Book, New York, NY, 1993

Napier, Nancy J., *Getting Through The Day*,
   W.W. Norton & Company, New York, London, 1993

Reeve, Christopher, *Nothing is Impossible,*
   Random House of Canada Limited, Toronto, 2002

Sanford, Linda Tschirhart, *The Silent Children,*
   Anchor Press/Doubleday, Garden City, NY, 1980

Sark, *A Creative Companion,*
   Celestial Arts, Berkeley, California,1989

Siegel, Bernie S., *Love, Medicine & Miracles,*
   HaperCollins Publishers, New York, New York

Truman, Karol K., *Feelings Buried Alive Never Die...,*
   Olympus Distributing, Nevada, 1991

Whitfield, Charles L., *Memory and Abuse,*
   Health Communications, Inc., 1995

Williams, Margery, *Velveteen Rabbit,*
   Bantum Doubleday Dell, 1922 and 1991

INDEX

A

Abandoned, 89
Abandonment, 129
    partner, 128
Addiction, 33
Adolescent After Effects, 26
Adult Children of Abusive Parents, 55
Advantages of Using Spiritual Beliefs,
    154
Agoraphobia, 28, 32
Always Call Me Daddy, 88
Anger, 45, 68, 70, 71, 83, 99, 109, 113,
    114, 136
Anguish, 14, 138, 152
Anorexia nervosa, 30
Antidepressants, 40, 50, 51
Anxiety, 12, 26, 27, 39, 45, 46, 50, 56,
    60, 72, 75, 77, 79, 93, 110, 149, 151,
    152, 154, 170
    release, 77
    separation, 27
Apologize, 85
Arnold Chiari Malformation, 34
Assault, 8
Assertiveness, 100

B

Becoming Real, 100
Bernie Siegel, 141
Bible, 70, 92
Black Hats, 108
Blue Ribbon Recipients, 124
Boundaries, 21, 66, 90, 129, 133
Breakthrough, 14, 48, 147
Broderick, Dr. Carlfred, 68

C

Center for InnerChange, 40, 73, 154. See
    Resources
Changing the Abuse Cycle, 116
Child abuse, 87, 112, 129, 167
    definition, 113
Childhood sexual abuse. *See* CSA

Children, 98
Chutis, Laurieann, flashback helps, 19, 20
Clergy, 134
Close Call, 46
Competence, 54, 78
Confidence, 17, 22, 67, 78, 89, 170
Courage
    during flashback, 24
    from moms, 84
    of friends, 127
    one of three C's, 132
    to continue program, 75
    to overcome phobia, 31
    to rappel, 60
    to talk, 83, 100, 135, 138
Crying, 93
CSA, 1, 13, 34, 36, 59, 71, 88, 123
    after effects, 25, 33
    clergy, 135
    denial, 16
    friends, 126
    helps for families, 85
    memory triggers, 44
    partners, 128
    patient, 140
    support persons, 124

D

Delight, 98
Denial, 16, 59
Depression, 8, 49, 51, 57, 72, 106, 110,
    129, 146, 168
    "no laughin" eyes, 49
    casualties of, 161
    chronic illness, 40
    common diagnosis, 145, 147, 151, 152
    teenage, 26, 30
Despair, 26, 39, 50, 75, 99
Disabled, 37
Disclosure, 34, 36, 83, 85, 88, 96, 129,
    145
Discovery, 11
    self, 12, 59

Discovery of my own abuse, 12
Dissociation, 44
Dominguez, Joe & Vicki Robin, 160
Dyslexia, 74, 170

E

Eating disorders, 29, 33, 163
Elgin, Suzette, 132
Emotional abuse, 112, 113

F

Family, 6, 14, 47, 54, 72, 81, 93, 108, 119
    adolescence, 27, 32
    dinner, 23
    gas leak, 37
    good times, 18, 65, 121
    mom on strike, 52
    physician, 34
    supportive, 156, 165
    troubled, 15
Fathers, 69, 88, 89, 92, 93, 94, 116
Fear - overcoming, 46, 47, 60
Flashback, 22, 23, 24, 30, 33, 65, 68, 75,
    82, 88, 90, 91, 98, 99, 102, 130, 147,
    148, 152, 161
    definition, 19
    helps, 20, 21
    support, 20
    The Return, 13
Forgiveness, 69, 70
Freedom, 5, 7, 11, 68, 100
Freedom to Create, 76
Friends, 72, 126

G

God, 44, 46, 56, 60, 69, 86, 98, 99, 111,
    136, 144, 155, 156
Granddaughter, 8
Grandfather, 5, 6
    letter to, 109
Grandfathers, 8, 70, 83, 91, 92, 105, 168
Grandmother, 7, 8, 22, 23, 34, 36
Grandmothers

letters to, 102, 104

Grandpa, 6
Groups. (*See* Therapy)

H

Healing Continuum, 75
Healing Process Timetable, 168
Hints for mothers, 85
Home Lab, 100
Hope, 1, 5, 35, 39, 48, 50, 66, 84, 108,
    130, 155, 161, 163
    The Secret Garden, 38, 39
Hug Power, 55
Husband, 13, 105, 119, 120
    as molester, 84, 109
    counseling, 118
    sex, 44
    support, 45, 52, 56, 61, 65, 70, 76, 150
    trails with, 99, 129, 130, 159
Hypnotherapist, 37, 47
Hysteria, 26, 34, 150

I

Illness, 41, 49, 51, 84, 113, 120, 129, 162,
    168
    abuse cycle, 163
    chronic, 72, 115
    during adolescence, *26, 27*
Incest, 19, 22, 45, 47, 49, 55, 68, 150,
    165
    clergy reactions, 135
    emotional, 94
    family affair, 108
    father-daughter, 88
    non-survivors, 161
    see VOICES, 124, 125
    Survivors of, 169
Intimacy
    sexual, 20, 43, 44

J

Joy, 23, 44, 51, 83, 84, 87, 127, 134, 135

Joyfulness, 36, 59, 76, 168

L

Latham, Glenn L., 119
Love, XI, 5, 9, 64, 65, 66, 79, 84
  fathers, 92, 93
  mothers, 86
  of family, 81, 93, 96
  of self, 14
  relaxation, 63
  sexual, 44
Love, Medicine and Miracles, 141
Love, Patricia, 94

M

Marriage, 5, 90, 128, 129, 130, 131, 132
Massage, 40, 56, 57, 147, 168
McDonald, Robert, 77, 86, 144, 158
Medication, 13, 23, 40, 41, 45, 64, 78,
  142, 156
Meditation, 154
Memory, 19, 83, 88, 155
  and hypnosis, 149
  childhood, 6, 8, 13, 82, 89
  flashback and, 19, 20
  in group therapy, 150
  true or false, 151
Mental Health Technicians, 139
Minson, Ron, 72, 73, 74, 75, 151, 163,
  169, 170
Miracles, 38, 74, 104
Monster, 75
Monsters, 30, 62
Mothers
  suggestions for, 85, 86
  two teachable, 84
Music and Miracles, 74
*My Parents Married on a Dare and Other
  Favorite Essays on Life*, 68

N

Nightmare, 7, 14, 30, 62, 78

NLP neurolinguistic programming, 17,
  77, 144

O

Obsessive Compulsiveness, 28
Options following flashbacks, 15

P

Panic attacks, 26, 28
Parents, To, 112
Partners, To, 128
Perpetrator, 20, 43, 60, 68, 69, 85, 88, 91,
  108, 109, 130, 131
Phobia, 26, 28
  School, 26
Physicians/Therapists, 141
Play, 27, 29, 39, 46, 64, 65, 75, 76, 87,
  115, 116
Positive Parenting Ideas, 118
Power of Positive Parenting, 119
Prayer, 35, 50, 62, 63, 92, 119, 126, 137,
  154, 155, 160
Pretending, 4
Progression, 74
Protection, 7, 18, 19, 45, 64, 91, 154
Psychiatrist, 27, 28, 32, 34, 35, 45, 47,
  72, 143, 150, 163
PTSD, Posttraumatic stress disorder, 145,
  147, 151, 163
Puzzle analogy, 18, 26

R

Rage, 99
Reaching Out, 37
Recapturing Delight, 64
Recovery, 1, 5, 15, 144
  accident related, 5, 47
  beliefs toward, 167
  chronology, 168
  emotional, 58, 123
  examples of, 126, 162
  family help, 86, 96, 100, 106
  in Denver, 163

journey, 53, 73, 76, 77, 157
laugh therapy, 121
medication, 51
of memory, 152
physical, 54, 59
process, 18, 22, 39, 59
spiritual, 68, 154
Relaxation techniques, 47
Religion, 44, 134, 135, 156
Respect, 78, 86, 94, 99, 113, 116, 131,
135, 138, 140, 141, 143, 166
Revenge, 1, 68
Rocovery
journey, 54

S

SARK, 76
Satir, Virginia, 115
Scars, 58
Self-Coaching, 79
Sexual Abuse, The, 5
Sisters, 95
Skinner, Valerieanne, II
Sleeping, 6, 40, 64, 120
Spanking, 116
Spiritual Recovery, 68
Stepfather, 32, 82, 88, 93
Struggle, XI, 23, 24, 130, 166
Suicidal, 17, 35, 161, 163
Survivor, 161

T

Terror, 12, 168
The Power of Positive Parenting, 119
Therapy, 39, 71, 72, 106, 121, 150
Art, 32
Group, 150
Laugh, 121, 160
Massage, 56
Music, 73
Non Group, 71
Physical, 40
Thriver, 163
Time out, 52

TLP, The Listening Program, 76. (*See* Resourses)
Tomatis Method, 170
Tonsil Party, 9
Touch, 16, 21, 34, 39, 54, 55, 63, 96, 141, 154
Touching, 12
Trauma, 1, 5, 7, 9, 19, 47, 50, 56, 71, 91, 93, 95, 143, 145, 165
as a trigger, 43, 46, 148, 149
at age 3, 4
effect of, 120, 130, 146
flashbacks, 19, 20
group therapy, 71
massage, 56
medication and, 142
return of, 13, 83, 99
teaching sessions, 84
Trauma Treatment and the Law, 151
validation, 85
Treasure, 66
Trigger, 20, 43, 44, 46, 83, 95, 142
True or False Memories. *See* memory
Truman, Karol K., 41
Trust, 50, 70, 124, 126, 139, 142, 151
and touch, 55
healing timetable, 168
in relationships, 131, 133
in the gender, 136, 142
in therapist, 141, 142, 145, 149
lack of, 4, 8, 9, 145, 147
physician, 35, 44, 75
poor choice, 47
to rappel, 61

V

Validated, 15, 50, 91, 100
Velveteen Rabbit, 100, 101
Victim, 31, 46, 164
and perpetrator, 108, 131
as survivors see Voices, 125
cycle, XII
following surgery, 45
forgiveness from, 70

helps for the relatives, 106
of abuse, 5, 7, 69, 145, 157, 158, 159,
    161
strengthening, 100, 136, 148, 157
Visualize, 111
VOICES in action, 124. (*See* Resources)

W

Whitfield, Charles, 151

Williams, Margery, 100
Withdrawing, 106
Wounds, 58, 59

Y

You Can't Say That To Me, 132
Your Money or Your Life, 160

Quick Order Form
Please Print

Fax orders: 801-383-7829   Send this form

Telephone orders: 425-338-4708   Have your credit card ready!

Email orders: victorialynn@aradiance.com

Postal orders: Aradiance Publishing, PO Box 13855, Mill Creek, WA, 98082

Please send the following books.
- ☐ Dear Sister, Once Abused $16.95
- ☐ Dear Sister, Once Abused Journal   (summer 2003)
- ☐ Hilda is Coming to Our House Today (summer 2003)

Please send more FREE information on:
☐ Other books ☐ Speaking/Seminars ☐ Fund Raising

Name: _____

Address: _____

City:_____State: _____Zip: _____

Telephone:_____

Email address: _____

Sales Tax: Washington State residents add 8.9% sales tax

Shipping by air:
U.S.: $4.00 for the first book and $.50 for each additional book.
International: $10.00 for the first book: $5.00 for each additional book.

Payment: ☐ Check   ☐ Credit Card ☐ Money Order
         ☐ Visa   ☐ Master Card ☐ AMEX ☐ Discover

Name on Card: _____

Card Number: _____Exp. Date: _____